UPDATED AND REVISED EDITION

Push Play

TAKING YOUR LIFE OFF PAUSE

TEXAS TITANS MEDIA, LLC

Texas Titans Media, LLC

Copyright © 2019 by Jason Wright

Published in the United States of America.

All rights reserved. No part of this book may be reproduced without permission from the author, except by a reviewer quoting brief passages in a review; nor may any part of this book be reproduced, stored in a retrieval system or copied by mechanical photocopying, recording or other means without written permission from the author.

Scripture taken from the Holy Bible, NEW INTERNATIONAL VERSION®, NIV® Copyright © 1973, 1978, 1984, 2011 by Biblica, Inc.® Used by permission. All rights reserved worldwide.

Produced with the assistance of Fluency Organization, Inc.

Graphic design: Inkwell Creative

To Jemilynn, Rylan, and Abby.
I love you more than everything.

TABLE OF CONTENTS

Preface 7

Chapter 1	I'm from the Future	9
Chapter 2	Why Do You Want More?	23
Chapter 3	Planning to Succeed	39
Chapter 4	What Freedom Affords	47
Chapter 5	Why Not You?	57
Chapter 6	Change: What A Scary Thing	69
Chapter 7	The Price of a Dream	81
Chapter 8	You, Inc.	91
Chapter 9	What We Really Want	101
Chapter 10	The Best Catastrophe That Ever Happened!	111
Chapter 11	It's Your Move	125
Chapter 12	Establish Your "Tribe of Mentors"	135
Chapter 13	Wanted: A Life	147

Suggested Reading 159
About the Author 161

PREFACE

A few years after I wrote the original edition of *Push Play* published in 2010, I found myself at a significant crossroads in my life. I had sold my real estate business, ran for Congress and lost, got divorced, and my daughters were about to leave for college. I didn't have a great fortune and had no ideas of how to obtain one. I was depressed and lost.

Then it happened.

I kid you not. I picked up a copy of my own book last year and realized I was becoming the guy who once told you all the great things you could do at any age and was now in the prime of his life just sitting back, wallowing in regret and self-pity. A 35-year-old Jason Wright got in the face of a 43-year-old Jason Wright and reminded him of who he was and what his capabilities were. I remembered I'd always wanted to write, encourage, and inspire others. There is simply nothing greater on this earth for me to do as a vocation.

It wasn't that I had regressed. I was the fact that I had chosen to forget a lot of the lessons I learned at 35. (Although I didn't know as much then as I thought I did!) If I didn't move quickly, I would prove myself ultimately a fraud and a loser. I had to act. I had to go forward. I had to create the Jason Wright I wanted to be, or rather the person I knew I was already but hadn't fully manifested.

So here I am, writing an updated edition of my first book. I'm back. I'm wiser. I'm much humbler. I'm now married to the girl of my dreams, who is proof every day of God's restorative nature. I have two amazing daughters in the blossom of their lives.

I want you to know these things upfront because I want to be transparent with you. I believe we often view authors and speakers as being superhuman. If I wrote a book on crushing life in my thirties, I must have it all figured out by now, right?

Heck no, I don't!

However, I will always use whatever gifts and talents I may possess to enrich the lives of others. If in doing so I have to expose some of my travels through dark valleys, I'm game. So with that disclosure, let's get going and "push play" on the lives we were meant to live.

CHAPTER 1
I'M FROM THE FUTURE

"Build this day on a foundation of pleasant thoughts. Never fret at any imperfections that you fear may impede your progress. Remind yourself, as often as necessary, that you are a creature of God and have the power to achieve any dream by lifting up your thoughts. You can fly when you decide that you can. Never consider defeat again. Let the vision in your heart be in your life's blueprint. Smile!"
—OG MANDINO, *A BETTER WAY TO LIVE*

Why are you here? No, I don't mean the physical location in which you currently find yourself. I mean, why are you holding this book? If it's because you want to break your life out of a holding pattern and start truly living, then I think you're in the right place.

I've been where you are. And now I'm not. I was no longer happy just "getting by" from one day to the next. So I did something about it. As a matter of fact, I've done several things:

- Bought a business that provides enough income that I don't have to have a "real" job
- Nailed almost perfect attendance at my daughters' school plays
- Became a pro-rated golfer on Wii (which is odd because I hate golf)

- Never travel on business, only for pleasure
- Am home every night
- Taught a Sunday school class
- Hiked the Himalayas (and almost died having one of the best experiences of my life)
- Went to the Beijing Olympics
- Served as president of my local Rotary Club
- Ran for Congress (lost)
- Got a divorce (Oh no)
- Got remarried (Boom!)
- Lost all my mojo (Uh oh)
- Found my mojo! (Boom!)
- Got my first paid keynote speaking gig!
- Learned who I am and what I really want to do with my life

Oh, and I've written a book (you're reading it). These are just some highlights of what I'm experiencing since making my decision to start living instead of just being alive, waiting to die. This is where I hope your focus will also be. Not thinking of ways to make more money. Not focusing on the short-term of what will make you happy. I want you to paint your own picture of what the rest of your life would look like—if you "pushed play" on your dreams and started really living. And then do it. I want you to begin thinking about a curated life. One where nothing is taken for granted and every moment, every material good, each relationship, goal, and ambition is in a place to reach its highest and best use.

I want this book to get you off-center. It's about gearing up and taking the leap of faith to pursue any dream you may have tucked away in your soul. You can do it. Yes, you can. Sorry to sound a little "cheerleaderesque" on you here, but it's true.

You also have to understand something about me that's going to come through in my writing. I despise victims. If thoughts like, "But Jason, you don't understand my situation..." or some other nonsense like that creep into your psyche, I want you to imagine me right in your face saying, "Shut your mouth and get to it." Of course, imagine me saying it with a little smile. I don't want you mad at me. I yelled at myself throughout this writing process, and the result is you're reading this book!

Whoever you are, wherever you are, whatever your circumstances, I believe you can achieve your goals so that you end up with a life you love. History is full of example after example of successful people who, deep down, were no different than you or me.

They just did things differently.

They saw the world differently

And, most importantly, they saw themselves differently.

You are not bound to a job or a life you hate. You were meant for more. There's a part of you that believes this, or you wouldn't have picked up this book.

So, let me ask you something. Are you willing to take the huge, necessary, and sometimes gut-wrenching steps it requires to take your life off pause and see what happens next? Whatever passion you have buried within you doesn't need to stay there any longer. If you are serious about loving your life and building your own wealth and independence, begin planning now. Start asking the right questions to help you reach your goals now. Become excited about your future life now. Once you grab the remote control of your dreams and push play, anything is possible.

MY STORY BEGINS

Do you remember answering the question, "What do you want to do when you grow up?" Well, you're grown up! What are you doing? If you don't like it, what are you going to do about it? So many people have hit the pause button on their dreams. They say they're waiting for the right time or the right circumstances. But somewhere along the way they just began waiting to die.

Of course, it's never the right time. There is always something standing in the way. The longer we wait to get our lives where we want them to be, the easier it is to put everything on pause. Putting it off will only keep it right there: off. If you continue looking for the perfect moment to arrive so you can finally live the life you want to live, you will be waiting from now on.

While I relate many of my life experiences throughout this book, this isn't about me. It's just the one illustration I have the most intimate knowledge of regarding this topic. I certainly haven't reached some level of greatness. To the contrary, I'm as normal as one can be.

I had a good-paying job with one of the largest companies in the world. Yet, I wanted out of my job. I couldn't get around the fact that I would never be happy working for someone else, because deep down I was an entrepreneur. So, I began planning my escape from "corporate America." The thing is, I wasn't Bill Gates. I didn't have a passion and/or hobby that I could turn into the world's greatest software. I just have a heavy dose of "I can do anything," even if I don't know exactly what the "thing" is. Oh, and there is the most powerful ingredient of all: faith.

When I say that I didn't have a passion or hobby to convert into a business, I mean it. Everyone around me thought I had this great business mind. That's not true. I was just good at business. I was also an All-State football player and went to college on a full-ride scholarship. But I hated football. In other words, just because you're good at something doesn't mean you like it. That was me. It's important that you realize this before you read my story. I wasn't looking to let some innovative idea out of a box. I was searching for a life. I refused to accept that a mediocre existence was all I was destined to live.

I've never been good at depending on others to determine my fate. I want ultimate control over that. In the rat race, you're at the mercy of many factors over which you have no control. That never sat well with me. I didn't want to depend on a 401(k), Social Security, long term health benefits, or any other trappings. I wanted to create a life of independence, not dependence.

And I got there.

I fully executed on my own "Push Play" moment years ago, succeeded, in many ways failed, and made it back. There have certainly been some bumps along the way. However, these days, business and work are a means to an end. It's what finances the things I want to do in life. I don't obsess and kill myself over work. Instead, I keep my focus on what work will allow me to be free to do when the time comes. How did all these tremendous changes come about? You'll have to read the rest of my story to find out.

A MESSAGE TO YOU AT ANY AGE

I'm approaching my mid-forties. I wrote the first version of *Push Play* when I was 35. With nearly another decade under my belt, I want to write to the decades I've experienced and hopefully impart some wisdom. After all, they say hindsight is 20/20. If you are in your 50s or 60s, I have a message for you as well, although I haven't caught you yet!

The 20s

To the 20-somethings I say, congratulations. You have no idea how lucky you are right now. You have the whole world before you. What's more, you have several mulligans to cash in yet. (That's a do-over in golf terminology.) There's not much you can do in your career that people won't overlook due to your age. When I was in my 20s I job-hopped like crazy. Mind you it never occurred to me to give deep thought to what I wanted to do and where I wanted to end up. I was playing to my ego and looking for a job that made me sound important and one that made me feel good about myself.

If I had it to do over, I would do it much differently. I would take a look at the landscape and think of what it was I wanted to do. I would dream crazy big dream, and I would—at a minimum—try to follow them. When I was in my 20s, I eliminated potentially good opportunities if I thought everyone else was pursuing them. For example, I played fullback instead of trying for quarterback in school because I assumed everyone wanted to be the quarterback, which I told myself meant I couldn't play that position. This negative mindset carried over to the jobs I pursued. I didn't take inventory of my gifts and talents, much less give myself credit for them enough to step out and stake my claim on a career I would enjoy.

You, my friends, are living in the most exciting and opportunity-filled times I've ever seen. It has never been easier to turn your passion into a vocation, and I don't just mean through traditional capitalistic endeavors. There are over 1.5 million nonprofits in operation in the United States at the time of this writing. Don't see the one that fits your passion? Start it. Thanks to social media and an ever more socially conscience populous, there has never been a better time to start a nonprofit.

Try new things. Your 20s are a time for you to experiment. Some of you will find your lane right away. Others will find it by trial and error. The point is you have to go for it. Start right now pursuing what you were made to do. It only gets harder the older you get. Embrace not having the car you want or the house, apartment, or condo you want. You're in your 20s. Nobody expects you to have nice stuff yet. Put your head down and work. Work your tail off and try as many things as you can for the first five to seven years of your career. Leave nothing to regret. It will fly by faster than you think.

Watch and learn. I'm a huge fan of YouTube and Instagram. These two platforms allow the brightest humans on earth to become teachers to those of us willing to listen. Guys like Tim Ferriss, Gary Vaynerchuk, Sam Harris, and Jordan Peterson are all sitting in a virtual 24-hour classroom ready to teach any willing student. All of these guys either have their own show and/or frequently appear on podcasts. They share their wisdom and disciplines for free. There is a never-ending well of information out there for the taking. Go get it. And remember, as hard as it is, to be patient. You have so much time. I used to put ridiculous arbitrary timelines on myself. Don't. Be patient and wait for your crops to grow. The more patient you are, the greater the harvest. I promise.

Do something that deserves being rewarded. Otherwise, shut up. This isn't the NFL where it's encouraged and accepted to celebrate for merely doing your job. I get frustrated watching NFL players make a tackle and run, dance, and jump around as though they had done something extraordinary. You did your job, bro! That's it. That's why you have so many zeros at the end of your freaking paycheck. It's your job to take down an opposing player. At the end of reading this book, my goal is for you to be inspired to do work that fulfills you and makes a real impact in our world.

The 30s

This is where things start to come into focus. I think my 30s were my most productive decade for sure. I held the same job, got elected to office, published a book, made decent money, and seemed to achieve whatever I put my mind to. However, I also sold my first business, got a divorce, and went to work for the government. By the time I was 40, I was pretty much doing nothing I could be proud of.

Embrace your youth. Your 30s are similar to that point in any endeavor where you're not quite halfway finished so you have a real option of changing course without too many ramifications. You still have some immaturity, but you're also wiser than you were in your 20s. People trust you more, but they also treat you with novelty due to your youth. Your ego may rear its head because of this. I remember as a business owner I was always trying to let people know that even though I was young, I deserved to own my business. I thought I had to prove my competence as a way to get respect. Don't do that. Be respected for your work. If someone who is your senior treats you as being young, that's okay. You are. Embrace it. Take advantage of the fact they are wiser than you, and learn from them. If you ask, 99% of the time they will guide you and help you. Don't miss out on the mentoring people are willing to give you. It's much weirder to be in your mid-40s asking people only five years older than you to be a mentor. Therefore, while you're young, get over yourself. Embrace the fact you don't know it all, and be willing to learn all you can. It's a great time. I loved my 30s.

Here's something I've noticed about today's world that's pretty amazing. When our ancestors were in their 30s, they were in the prime of their life. Did you know Jesus was only 33 when he died? Thomas Jefferson was the same age when America won her independence. When he penned the

Declaration of Independence, he was also a mere 33 years old. Most of the Founding Fathers barely had 20 more years to live. Our founders were very young compared to today's political leaders. By their mid-20s they were already setting the course for a new nation. They were thought leaders. They were fully running in their lane.

Then came the 20th century when we started to live a little longer. Men basically just put their head down and ground it out for 30 years, and then they hung it up to play golf or fish out their golden years. What else were they going to do? The world communicated with them through the newspaper and three TV stations. If these men had a message for the world, there was no feasible way for them to get that message out. So they just worked—and smoked, drank, and retired.

The world today is reminiscent of the early days of America. The new economy has allowed for 20- and 30-somethings to be as accomplished as our forefathers. It's just not unusual to pick up the paper and read about another 30-year-old billionaire. That same 30-year-old will soon go on to be a 36- year-old thought leader in politics, human rights, and social awareness. Furthermore, unlike our forefathers, this individual then probably has 50 more years to be active in the world.

Be patient. I've noticed and somewhat fallen victim to an unrealistic sense of urgency. We hear about Elon Musk, Jeff Bezos, Mark Zuckerberg, Whitney Herd, Ryan Holiday, Peter Thiel and the list goes on of young billionaires and think we should be getting our windfall sooner. We see people in their late 20s and early 30s living amazing lives on social media, seemingly crushing it. No wonder we think we're falling behind.

I have some news for you. The reason we all know the big names listed above is because they are outliers. They are the extreme rarity of the business world. As for the folks on social media, most of them are making their life up on their phone. Theodore Roosevelt once said, "Comparing oneself to others is a thief of joy." It is, so don't do it. Reading the insights and principles in this book will hopefully inspire you to just be you.

Identify your lane. By your 30s you should have your lane clearly identified. If you don't, what are you doing to rectify that? You still have so much time to jump in and run. I remember having this stupid arbitrary deadline in my head to be "accomplished" by the time I was 40. I actually wanted to be able to retire by 40. I have no idea why. I just did, and that was stupid. I spent so much time worrying I wasn't in the right lane that I never focused on the one I was in. Please don't do that. If you can figure out in your 30s you're in the lane you're supposed to be in, that's amazing. Embrace it and crush it. If you're not, take time to meditate on your desires, your talents, and your ambitions. More on that in later chapters.

The 40s

It was in my 40s that I actually picked up a copy of my first edition of this book and read it. I was in a wilderness of sorts at that time, and I needed a major kick in the pants. The 35-year-old Jason gave 43-year-old Jason that very thing. It's a very odd thing when your own book works on you. It's a weird way to do research and development, and I don't recommend it!

Don't be ruled by fear. The 40s is a scary time. However, it's also an incredibly amazing time. We have been so programmed to believe that 40 is the middle of our life. I don't believe that. The middle is later now. There's just too much evidence to prove it. At the time of this writing, we have a president who very well may be pushing 80 when he leaves office. We have a Commerce Secretary who is 80. Warren Buffett is 87 years old! His long time business partner Charlie Munger is 94! I don't think many of us can imagine Berkshire Hathaway annual meetings without these two titans at any age. More and more people are refusing to hang it up.

They just keep going and going. The thing that angers me the most about the perception of 40 is it's supposed to somehow be the end of youth. I think this is what puts many in a tailspin. I've been seeing this ad on Instagram that reads, "Fit after forty." What the heck? Why wouldn't I be fit after 40? Forty is not old anymore. I know it has at times been hard for me to deal with the fact that I'm in my 40s. However, I refuse to accept that it's the end of my youth. In fact I had a great epiphany today. As I was driving down the road, I saw a shopping center and remembered eating there with a friend at a burger joint when we were in junior high.

I thought about those times and realized nothing much had changed. I still felt the same, but I'm smarter. I'm wiser, and I have a little more money. My mind is still alert enough to take me back to that very day we ate burgers, so why couldn't I still embrace that youthfulness? I can! I simply refuse to accept age as a thing. Why should I? Why should you? If you are still physically and mentally able to do 80-90% of what you want, why in the heck wouldn't you? It's only going to be harder tomorrow, next week, a month, or a year from now—so do it! Go! Act as young as you feel.

Act with urgency and patience. The fact is, you and I have no idea how much more time we have. Therefore, we may as well act with urgency and patience at once. This book will show you how. Don't waste a single day, but remember there's still runway left. This has been one of the greatest realizations of my life. I thought my life was over at 40. I thought whatever I was at 40 was it. That's who I was. That's how wealthy or not wealthy I was. I lived with this mindset that everything operated from a fixed position. I refuse to do that any longer. I'm living as though I have all the time in the world, but it could also be the end of the world. I think this mindset helps me to enjoy the journey. When you don't beat the heck out of yourself for not meeting some arbitrary deadline, you can then just enjoy the process.

I have a drop-dead date to complete this book, but I'm not going to sweat it. I'm going to pound out as much as I can day after day and remember how fun it is still having the fruits of my labor to look forward to. I think we all need to remove this notion of quitting, or the better and more used term, "retiring." If your engine still hums, then keep getting on the track of life. You still have much to offer no matter your age.

The 50s and Beyond

Remember, age is just a number. I'm only 43, so I'm going to be writing purely from theory as opposed to experience on the following age set. All I can say is every passing year I have more and more respect for older people who are out there still crushing it. I love to visit with an older person who still speaks as though they are 30 years younger. Have you noticed this? These are the people who, if you close your eyes and listen to them, you'd never know their age. It's because their speech has a clarion quality. Their minds are sharp. They have great things to say, and they say them well.

A perfect example of this is legendary basketball coach George Raveling. Raveling is 80 years old and active as ever. This is a man who by all accounts could have considered his career complete and gone on to retire to a life of leisure long ago. However, at the age of 80 he is still crushing it every day at Nike. He has a storied career that includes such accomplishments as receiving the John W. Bunn Lifetime Achievement Award and the Lapchick award, as well as being inducted into the Naismith Memorial Basketball Hall of Fame. Raveling could easily have just sat back and rested with the assurance he had lived life well. Another little known fact is Raveling was present at Martin Luther King's "I have a dream" speech during the march on Washington. Raveling, was there thanks to the financial assistance of a mentor, and he actually met Dr. King and asked for a copy of the speech King took to the podium with him. Dr. King gave it to him, and Raveling to this day owns this incredible artifact from one of America's most historic moments.

In 1994 after retiring from coaching basketball, Phil Knight of Nike called Raveling and asked him to take a job with him. He wanted the coach to become Nike's Global Basketball Sports Marketing Director, and Raveling has done so ever since. This is a man who at 57 was set to retire. However, it turns out it was just his rookie year as a corporate executive. Most people are looking to end a career at 57, not start one. This was not the case with Raveling.

Over and over at different points in this book, I mention the ever-energetic and seemingly never-slowing entrepreneur Gary Vaynerchuk. Gary Vee, as he's often referred to, constantly takes issue with people who use their age as an excuse to stop executing or rather, as he calls it, "deploying their craft." The market doesn't give a rip how old the owner of an Etsy store is. The market doesn't care how old the producer of Ryan Serhant's vlog is. If you haven't watched Ryan's vlog, you should. The market does not care about your age. The market only cares about the value you add to the lives that comprise that market.

Make good choices. Life is about choices in your 50s and beyond. You will make good ones, and you will make bad ones. Lord knows I've made plenty of the latter. I advised my daughter Rylan when she was 18 that she could completely bypass the traditional route of getting on ESPN. You can also get to your desired destination in more than one way. It's up to you—not society, your boss, your wife, your kids, or anyone else to determine when you have no utility value left. Only you can decide that. I assure you, in fact I promise you, there's a ton more left in you than you realize. We'll talk in detail about this in later chapters.

My dad frustrates me to no end. Don't get me wrong. I love him. He's an incredible guy. In 1991 Dad was diagnosed with macular degeneration. This is a disease that attacks the central vision. Essentially all the cells that reproduce to keep your central vision functioning stop reproducing. As of today Dad is only left with his peripheral vision.

Dad was a homebuilder like my grandfather before him. He was a good one, too. In fact, he was so good he would turn business away. Better yet, people would wait as long as a year for my dad to build their home. About 10 years ago he reached a point where he could no longer drive because of this disease. Therefore, it wasn't long after that when he quit building altogether. What frustrates me is the fact that all that institutional knowledge is still there inside my dad's brain. My Dad still knows what it takes to build a custom home. His mind is as sharp as ever. However, he has convinced himself that his utility value is so low. All that knowledge and wisdom is sitting unused in this critical space.

Now my dad is bored. He often sits alone on our farm in Sulphur Springs with little to do but take care of his dog, Lucy. I hate this for him. It breaks my heart to know he has so much to offer, but he's not deploying his skills. I've suggested a number of times my partnering with dad and building again. I know nothing about building a house, and the thought of doing it scares me to death. However, I know with my dad's guidance I could do it. The conversation always ends up Dad telling me all the reasons someone shouldn't build in this day and age (all the while, other builders are building all the new homes in Sulphur Springs my dad is fully capable of constructing).

I'm not bashing Dad. He's one of a million people just like him. He doesn't realize the utility value he still possesses. That's because he's never audited it against the market. Have you done this? Have you stepped outside yourself and performed a serious audit and accounting regarding all your years of work and the knowledge you've gained and then looked for a place in the market to deploy it? There are a million doors to consider walking through today where once there were only a few. But you must make the decision to look for them.

Honestly, I doubt there will be a lot of folks over 60 who pick up this book. However, many of you reading this have parents like my dad. You know they have something to offer. They have their eyesight and health, yet they are doing nothing with these resources. I bet some of your parents are also battling depression. I am of the belief that there is nothing better to help cure depression for older folks than finding a useful purpose for their talents.

My former father-in-law took early retirement from Shell Oil as an environmental attorney. While he was only 55 and at the top of his game, he decided he didn't want to do anything law-related. But he stayed busy and almost immediately became a volunteer at the Houston Symphony. He has one of the most incredible libraries of classical CDs I've ever seen. It has to rival the greatest collections of the most well-stocked libraries. By volunteering for the symphony, he was able to not only feed his love of classical music but also deploy his knowledge of the genre to patrons in a way he never had as an attorney.

That's not all. The guy also decided to start volunteering at Estes Park every year in Colorado. Every summer around August he heads to the mountains to volunteer at the YMCA camp up there. Oh, but there's more! He is also a volunteer at the Houston Museum of Natural Science and the Houston Arboretum. He stays busy sometimes as much as seven days a week.

Although he doesn't make a dime for these activities, he's being productive. This may not seem like a hustle to you, but I think it might be one of the greatest ones there is. What he's not making in cash, he's making in adding more years to his time on earth.

I once gave a speech to a group during the financial crisis of 2008. I titled it, "The Sun Came Up and There's Work to Be Done." I described to the audience that while times were challenging, there was still work to be done. It's the same with you. There's a day for things to get better. Your age is a number, but it pales in significance to your utility value. As long as the sun comes up, there's work for YOU to do. Go get it. Audit yourself and deploy your utility. I'm still pushing play, and I hope you will do so at any age. Let's go!

TIME TO GET REAL

1. How have you let your age limit your goals? Be specific.
2. Take some time to identify and negative, restrictive thinking in any areas of your life as it relates to age.
3. How would you fill in the blanks in this sentence? "Because I am [your current age] , I don't believe I can _____ ." Why are you letting this belief hold you back?
4. When was a time you did *not* let your age shape your goals?

CHAPTER 2
WHY DO YOU WANT MORE?

"What I really lack is to be clear in my mind what I am to do, not what I am to know...The thing is to understand myself, to see what God really wishes me to do...to find the idea for which I can live and die."

—SOREN KIERKEGAARD

If you're in a quandary about what to do next in your life, I'm sure you've probably heard everyone's opinion on what you *should* do. But whose advice should you listen to most?

Before we even get into that, let's take a deep breath. I think I (and anyone else) would be setting you up for failure if we tried to look at your life in total at this point. I firmly suggest starting with small things in incremental quantities. For example, if I tell you to "get healthy," what does that mean? Your answer would surely contain something about proper diet, exercise, and maybe some habit breaking. Left to your own devices, you might then list all the things you believe need to be done to become healthy. I can almost guarantee that you would soon fail in executing this list and quickly return to all your old habits. However, imagine if I suggested you do three pushups per day this week. "That's it. Just start there," I'd say. "In a week we'll make another change." This approach would allow you to master one incremental change before adding another, thereby increasing your likelihood for success. So when we start to look at "what is next" in your life, we need to start with a simple, executable strategy.

A mentor once illustrated this truth to me. Let's say I come to you for advice about chest pains I've been having. You listen politely and suggest I take two aspirin before bed for a week. That's fine if you happen to be a doctor, but what if you are a CPA by training and the only medical training you've had is from watching *Grey's Anatomy* episodes on TV? A simple answer such as taking two aspirin before bed just isn't going to cut it. Let's say, however, that you happen to be a heart surgeon and you give me the same advice. It's still a simple answer, but now we're on the right side of complexity. As a physician, with a decade of medical training under your belt, you've earned the ability to address a complex issue like a potential heart problem with a simple solution like taking two aspirin. Therefore, simplicity on that side of complexity is satisfactory.

There are two points I want to make here. First, the solution to getting health, making money, and finding your joy all start with one simple change at a time. Don't try to tackle the whole mission at once. Second, when mapping out the course, seek advice and guidance from those who have performed well and have earned credibility.

So, why should you listen to these simple truths I'm sharing with you? I'm on a different side of complexity than many of you are. After I had been in business for myself about a year, I started writing this book. Only I soon realized I was in no position to do that! I had not yet dealt with many of the complexities that would come after nearly a decade of self-employment. I'm trying to make a complex principle simple. When you strike out on a broad subject like changing your life, it often invites a bunch of psychobabble nonsense, and that's just not what you're going to get from me. I'm actually going to tell you how to do this.

This book has taken me almost two decades to write. Much like all our lives, this book is a work in progress even after I publish it. I will most likely build upon it in the future. While I've done all I can to gather the richest experiences and teachings I've gleaned over the past 20-plus years, I know there is more to learn and share. I will continue to do all I can to give you the best I have right now.

YOU MUST HAVE A WHY

Let's take a time-out from my story and talk about you for a moment. Why do you want to escape from your current situation? Are you looking for happiness in the form of a job? Give great attention to this question, and don't make a move until you can fully answer it. I remember how this haunted me when I made my leap. When I made my transition into entrepreneurship, I hated my job. I can't even begin to tell you how much I hated my work at that point.

The thing that scared me, and here is where I want you to take note, was whether or not I was leaving my safe corporate job for the right reason. Was I running from a job I didn't like? Was I just following my old pattern of looking for happiness in the form of a job? It was so hard to tell. My discontent had grown to the point where I was tempted to get a job at Starbucks or maybe even as a ditch digger. I just wanted to get out of what I was doing, but I also knew how critical this move was for my family and for me.

I had been negotiating the purchase of my first company for almost six months. I had no idea how I would pull it off. I didn't have a high net worth to speak of, and I had no family money to fall back on. I was not what you would call a finance genius with a trick up my sleeve. I was making $70,000 per year as an executive trainee for the Home Depot Corporation. However, I wanted to own my own business.

Why did I want to own my own business? Well, let me take you through a typical day as a member of the Store Leadership Program launched by then HD CEO Bob Nardelli. I had been given the task of learning and understanding the construction business of Expo Design Center. For those of you who don't remember Expo, it was a high-end design studio and retail store. It was like Pier One on steroids and was also a remodeling business.

Nevermind that I had never performed any kind of construction in my life. Here I was responsible for managing our in-house contractors. I would drive across town 45 minutes each way to get to my office located inside the store. I had to be there to open the store, so this meant getting up at 4:30 a.m. just to get there on time for the stocking associates to get in and begin their day before customers showed up. It was absolutely miserable. Besides having to schlep across town every day six days per week to get to my vocation, I also traveled like a madman. It was not unusual for me to travel to Atlanta, Georgia, and Irvine, California, multiple times per month. This schedule left little to no time with my daughters, Rylan and Abby. I hated this job. I still hate that job. A close friend of mine named Cullen also worked there with me, but neither of us could stand this awful place. But it's where we were for this time in our life.

I knew I was capable of doing something more, and I also knew I was destined to do it. Why? I wanted a life. "If the why is big enough, the how is usually not a problem," says entrepreneur Merry Riana. The answer to my "why" was I wanted a life that looked the way I wanted it to look. It wasn't more money that was my "why." It wasn't even being overly passionate about my vocation. It was a vision of a life I wanted to live.

THE VISION TAKES SHAPE

Leader and visionary Andy Stanley writes, "Vision is born in the soul of a man or woman who is consumed with the tension between what is and what could be. Anyone who is emotionally involved—frustrated, brokenhearted, maybe even angry—about the way things are in light of the way they believe things could be, is a candidate for a vision. Visions form in the hearts of those who are dissatisfied with the status quo."

In Andy Stanley's book *Visioneering* he also lists two important questions we must ask before casting our vision. The first is, "What difference will it make?" You must in painstaking detail list out what will happen if you make this move, change, quit this job, ask this person to marry you, etc. Whatever the move is, be able to completely answer what difference it will make if you take the leap, as well as what will be the difference if you don't.

The second question is, "Why should I attempt this?" This is huge. The question forces us to be honest with ourselves. Should you do it because you have the talent? Should you do it because your family's well-being hinges on it? Why should you do it? Ask yourself this question over and over until you feel you've completely exhausted the biggest why.

Before I even packed a single box at my office, I started to evaluate how my life as a whole would look if I made the change. I saw a much shorter commute. I could see myself diving headfirst into a community and not just being an anonymous human lost in a sea of faces. I pictured one day walking my kids to school. I also saw building a team of professionals with the skills and acumen I admired. I imagined taking a firm to the next level. I pictured poring through my own P&L and finally doing sales forecasts for my own shop. Man, it started to look good.

To me, the idea of watching *The Great Outdoors* on TV in my office on Saturday morning exemplified more than a luxury. It was freedom. It was a cool picture on several levels. First of all, the thought of working on a Saturday didn't bother me at all. Second, it meant I could pursue a long-shelved interest in hunting that I had not indulged in since I was in high school. More than that, in this grand vision of my future life, it was my company and I had a TV in my own office. Yea baby!

Again, money was never the concern. I knew if I bought a company, I could expect to suffer financially for a while. But I honestly believed the lifestyle would make up for the lack of funds. Self-employment and entrepreneurship outweighed the money issue. After some serious soul-searching, I realized that I was no longer running *from* my job, but running *to* something I desperately wanted.

I heard that about developing a vision board, so I came up with one but rarely gave it a thought. I didn't illustrate my vision properly. To me just putting pictures of "stuff" you want to have wasn't very motivating. However, that's exactly what I did when I made my vision board. I would warn you against doing the same thing. It's not about setting goals to obtain stuff. It's about creating a vision for what is behind those things.

For example, if I asked you why you wanted the big house in the picture on your vision board, what would your answer be? After all, a house is a house is a house at the end of the day. They all have walls, ceilings, plumbing, and the like. So what is it about one that's bigger and more well-appointed that makes you want it? What if you get the big house and find out that I was right: a house is, in fact, a house regardless of how big and fancy?

I don't think your vision should be so much about stuff as it should be about experiences. When gaining new experiences becomes the focus, we will often find the cost is much less than what we anticipated. All the "stuff" we thought we needed to bring about those experiences is not needed at all.

This was the case for me when I decided to move to a world of self-employment. I envisioned the life of freedom and independence I would have. It was this vision that drove me forward, not the hopes of material wealth.

LOOK BEFORE YOU LEAP

Now let's look at your circumstances. Why are you reading this book? Why are you considering a change? Does self-employment sound good because you won't have to deal with your boss anymore? You won't have to deal with all those late-night work sessions that benefit someone else's company? Maybe you're not an entrepreneur, but do you ever wonder about changing entire careers so you can finally find out if you'd be good at something else? Those may be good reasons. I honestly don't know. Your reasons might carry much greater weight with you than with me.

Is it wealth you are after? Do you want to be a millionaire? If so, why? I doubt very seriously that it's because you like to collect little green sheets of paper with presidents' pictures on them. No, the reason you want the million is because of the life you think it will give you. That's precisely where the focus needs to be. You must figure out the real drive behind your discontent with the status quo. If you dig deep enough, you're likely to find that life may only require you to make $45,000 a year changing the lives of children in a classroom than making a million dollars doing something else.

Here is the buzz phrase of this chapter, so go ahead and grab your highlighter. The best way to bring clarity to this situation is to ask, "Am I running from my current job, or am I running to a better life I know I'm capable of living?" Running from something is exhausting. When you finally reach so-called safety, you're tired. And wherever you are, there you are. Nothing has changed. Your life hasn't changed, just your geography.

If you're running from and not to, then put on the brakes and stay put for a while. I was running to a better life as I saw it. I had been on the run from jobs my whole career. This was the first time I ever ran to something else. More importantly, I was running toward a dream and a better life. Even a prisoner who plans to escape is running to something. My guess is that what motivates him most is not the cold prison that he's running from as much as it is the freedom he is running to.

If you are merely running from the job and end up as an entrepreneur, here is what can happen. You just might find out that you don't like where you find yourself. Again, wherever you go, there you are. The only difference is now you are responsible for much more than you were in your old job. Now you are the head man or woman, and your new company might be what supports a family other than yours. If it turns out that you don't like being on your own, you won't be successful, and you run the risk of failure. That would mean you now have the stigma of failing at the first company you ever ran.

This is important to realize because even the most passionate and smartest of entrepreneurs often fail. So, what are the odds that you will succeed, if you really aren't even happy about what you are doing?

Obviously, there is no quiz that's going to indicate if you're going to like it when you move forward. That would be too easy, and it would leave out the element of faith. No, the checklist is in your heart and soul, in places no one else can see. You have to go there to decide what your real motivation is. When you get there, listen. Be honest with yourself. Don't be discouraged if you conclude that you're not ready. Expect to face doubts, but most importantly be honest with yourself.

Let me ask you something. Does it make you insane every time you have to do something the "company" way, when you know you could do it better? Do you stay up at night with ideas racing through your head that you know if you could just get the higher-ups to listen to and sign off on would make the company a ton of money? Do you feel like someone just kicked you in the stomach every time you pull out of the driveway to head to the airport and your children are waving goodbye knowing they won't see Mommy or Daddy again until next Tuesday? Have you invented the next Windows software and you are ready to secure venture capital and get into full development? Would you like to be a PTA mom, but you can't squeeze it in because of the job you hate?

There are lots of questions to consider, and only you know the answers. More important, only you know the right questions that will grab your attention. What are you going to do about it? For the love of your family, know that you know, that you know, why you are stepping out. Don't climb Mt. Everest unless you've trained and can run a mile with an oxygen mask on. And even if you've trained for 20 years while holding your breath for a mile, if you are afraid of heights and don't like cold—don't go. Just because you're physically prepared won't be good enough. You have to have something burning deep inside that tells you that your world is never going to be right unless you get to the top of that mountain.

You must believe, without a shadow of a doubt, that failure is not an option. If you think getting to the top of that mountain will give you all you ever wanted in life and more, then you will do whatever it takes to get ready to go. You will purposely take on frostbite. You will deal with lack of oxygen. You will run and climb until you're dizzy, because you are running to something greater than all that pain: the top of the mountain. Oh, and remember, it's going to be hard. It's going to be very, very hard, but in the end, you'll be on top of the world. If you believe that end exists, then saddle up cowboy.

On the other hand, if all you can come up with is that it would just be a cool story for the grandkids about how grandma or grandpa started a company, then you will most likely never make it to the mountaintop. And guess what? You will be just fine staying at sea level.

If it sounds like a good idea to make a change and you find yourself saying, "Well, it would have to be better than this," let me tell you this: it won't be. However, if you can't sleep at night from thinking of how exciting it would be if tomorrow you woke up and went to your own company with your own coffee maker and your employees and your own vision...then guess what? It will be!

DON'T BE AFRAID OF BUTTERFLIES

Is fear the one thing stopping you? If you aren't grappling with a little fear, there might be something wrong with you.

I recently heard comedian Brian Regan say something about fear that stuck with me. Regan advised a group of would-be comedians, "Don't be afraid of the butterflies. Most of the best things in life happen after the butterflies."

Now he should know something about fear. Stand-up comics are some of the bravest humans there are. First, we've all heard the old data point that more people are afraid of death than public speaking. I'm not sure that's even true any longer, but for the sake of making this point, let's say it is. Imagine getting up in front of group of strangers who have paid money to see you and with that payment said non-verbally, "Now make me laugh." That's pressure, and it requires a certain modicum of bravery.

It's what happens after the butterflies that counts.

HOW DID I DO IT?

I have much more understanding and respect for those of you who are at the so-called mid-point of life. When I left Home Depot, I was 28. Let's face it. If I had bombed and lost everything, I still had plenty of time to recover. An older and wiser Jason is here to tell you, I get it. It's not the same.

The runway for the 50-year-old making a change is shorter. What this story describes is a 28-year-old who didn't know enough yet of what to fear, so he wasn't afraid. And I purposefully kept it the way I wrote it at 28 so you could see that I was as much naïve as I was cocky. I was as much desperate as I was hopeful. The point is this comes off as a story of confidence and bravado. It's not. It's a pre-30-year-old who in many ways was just lucky to have the right internal vision mixed with the right circumstances to push me off the diving board.

That said, I'm now the mid-lifer myself. I'm starting over again in a way. While I'm not looking to start another traditional business, I am trying to make a full-time business out of doing what I love, which is to write, speak and inspire. I told my youngest daughter, Abby, when I decided to pursue this endeavor that I felt as if I was joining the circus. Being a public speaker and writer isn't a real job. However, I'm here. You and I are here together. We're trying to figure this thing out. My hope is some of what I've done from 28 to now gives you a nudge and a little insight to do whatever it is you need to do to enhance your life experience. With that disclaimer, please read on.

So, now you know why I did it. But many of you may be asking the same question: how. "How did you do it, Jason? How did you, at 28, just up and leave a Fortune 500 career, move to a new city, and make your first company acquisition?" Even if you aren't asking the question, I believe you will enjoy hearing the rest of the story. So I'm going to tell you. Who knows? It might even give you some ideas for making your own jump.

First, you have to understand that as an entrepreneur, I think differently. I don't look at something and say, "Oh, I can't afford that." I look and say, "How do I get the money to buy that?" Then I act. These qualities led to me becoming an entrepreneur in the first place. There's something in me that always says of any problem, "There has to be a way to get this done. If someone else has done it, surely it can be done again by me." I do hope you grab on to that idea. There's nothing new under the sun. Whatever it is you are seeking out to better your life is absolutely possible. There are no guarantees, but if you truly know yourself and know what you are after is within reach of your physical and intellectual capabilities, it can be done. It might be hard, but there is a way. If there is an obstacle, then the obstacle merely becomes the way, as author and entrepreneur Ryan Holiday writes in his book, *The Obstacle Is the Way*. Philosopher Marcus Aurelius wrote about this centuries ago when he said, "The impediment to action advances action. What stands in the way becomes the way."

That's what happened with my first company. When I found out that a national real estate franchise was for sale, I wanted it. But I had to find a way to buy the company that didn't require a lot of cash because I simply didn't have a lot. Now, I will say that I had more than most. I started investing in the stock market and educating myself on investments right out of college. *Money Magazine* was the best textbook I ever owned. As a result, I saved and had a pretty good portfolio put together. However, I didn't have the money to go out and purchase a company. I had to make a deal.

I was looking at a $690,000 acquisition of the franchise and office building. Most median-income people would look at that figure and say, "Good lord. There is no way on earth I can pull that off." I didn't. The life I had painted in my mind (the why) was worth far more than $690,000. I asked myself, "How can I get the money to make this work?" For some reason, finance just makes sense to me. That's a funny thing too because I hate math. However, attach equity, interest, and leveraging to the numbers, and I "get it" most of the time.

Step 1: The Negotiation – First of all, I had to get the price down on the company. This was easy, because there is a standard formula used to evaluate the value of brokerage firms. With the assistance of some folks at the national franchise office, I negotiated the price down. Next, the building. I realized early on that the building was the key to this purchase.

I negotiated the acquisition down to the figure I had in mind. There was one problem though. How do I pay for it? Notice I didn't say, "I couldn't afford it." The capital was the obstacle, so "the way" was to find the capital by a means other than my bank account. If you want something badly enough, then you can and will make it happen. My wheels started turning.

One night on my way home from work in Houston, I was listening to a Carleton Sheets tape on how to buy real estate with no money down. The principle is simple. You use the owner's equity to make your down payment and get the owner to take a second lien.

Step 2: Revelation – The owners had told me that their building was almost paid for, so I saw some equity to work with. This is how the rich think, so pay attention. (I don't mean that to be smug; it's just a fact.) This is how you look at the money vault as half-full versus half-empty. I went to my local banker and asked him if he would loan me 50% of the value of the building. I would then pay off the owners' note and have money left over. I would use a portion of this money as an extra down payment on the franchise. I would then ask the owners to take a second lien on the building and finance the difference on the franchise.

This required some selling, as you might imagine, and I knew it. Therefore, I also took their interests into consideration. If I were them, what would I want? Well, first I wouldn't need all the money upfront. At the time, money market accounts were paying about 1.7% interest. I knew I could beat that return on a promissory note. Second, I knew they wouldn't like the tax burden they would incur. I also had to give them peace of mind.

If you want a seller to take a second lien, you better do a good sales job. The thought of a building that was nearly paid for now belonging to someone else and a bank in front of the seller in the instance of default is not easy for the seller to stomach. So, you ease the pain. I asked my banker to draft a legal document stating that in the instance of foreclosure, the owners would have first right of refusal to purchase the building from the bank for the balance of the note. Worst-case scenario, the owners get their building paid off with my credit, and then they turn around and buy back their building and sell it again to someone else. In the meantime, they would be collecting monthly payments from me of principal plus 8% interest.

I had to assure them that I was at least smart enough to make five years' worth of payment. Even if I defaulted after five years, they would get their building paid off. Plus, they'd have the money from my payments and could take the building back and then re-sell it. This plan set them up with a long term annuity that made for nice retirement income generated from their building.

Would I have done it? No. But let's remember which side of the deal I'm on.

So, there you have it. I purchased a company and a choice piece of commercial real estate with no money down and walked away from the closing table with almost $100,000 in my hand. Now that's a sweet deal. I convinced the owners to let me use the equity of their building to purchase their company from them. I fully realize my deal was a good one and not likely to happen every day. They put a great deal of trust in me and my ability to run the company and pay them back. I would say it worked out well for both of us. I was a big part of their retirement, and their former company was a big part of my future. It worked out great.

The financing I structured for this deal is not available on any banker's laptop for distribution. Most likely your local VP of commercial lending isn't going to sketch out this plan for you. However, don't assume if an idea is not easily accessible that it doesn't exist or that it's a bad idea. Sometimes you just have to be creative.

When I speak to groups, I like to have some fun. I tell the audience to raise their hands in the air as high as they can. I then tell them to raise them higher. Almost 100% of the room without fail lifts their hands just a tad higher than they did the first time. I do this to prove a point. Many things thought to be impossible are absolutely possible. Rarely is there only one way to complete a task.

Henry Ford had the idea of the V8 engine. He knew it would be a remarkable innovation and one that would forever change his automobiles. He assembled his best engineers and told them he wanted a more powerful engine with all eight cylinders cast in one block. They immediately told him it could not be done. There was no way to fit that sized motor into an automobile. Ford ignored their complaints and excuses and instructed them to get to work and to stay at it until they finished. It took two years for the engineers to come up with a design that would work, but after many failures and attempts, they finally succeeded.

This is the type of determination you must have. Whatever the big change in your life is, what you're looking for may not happen quickly. In fact, I can almost guarantee you it won't. There will be many obstacles along the way. Some will look like dead ends. Keep going. Keep pushing. Your desire for a better or different life must move from the "want" side of the ledger to the "need" side of the ledger. This requires looking into the future and making yourself face what life will look like if you don't achieve your desired change. Start now. Tony Robbins has a very useful exercise for this. Take out a pen and write down everything that *not* achieving this goal will mean. Then write down everything that achieving the goal will do to enhance your state of living. Make all those positives your drivers for success. Look at them every single day. Tattoo them on your brain.

So if going out and buying a business is the answer to your change, how do you do it? You first have to go look. Business brokers are everywhere, and there is always some family-owned business where the owner is sick and tired of running the shop. There are also companies out there where some smart turn-around artist has bought a business, brought it up to speed, and is now ready to sell it for a profit. The fact is that companies, much like houses, are always on the market even if they aren't technically "on the market." Catch a business owner on the right day, and she may almost throw you the keys and say, "Here, take it." You just have to go find them. Find one that meets your criteria and piques your interest. You would be amazed at how much some of the owners want to get out and, as a result, will sell you the business with sweet financing arrangements. Just be sure you know how to play the game of finance.

Once you find YOUR deal, have the determination of Henry Ford to make it happen. Don't accept no for an answer. Always bear in mind that just because someone doesn't possess some boilerplate template to execute your plan doesn't mean a new path cannot be charted. Sit down, think it through, and see if a solution presents itself. If it's not illegal, it's probably a possibility.

FINDING HAPPINESS

I eventually sold the real estate business in my thirties, but I was so happy when I left corporate America and transitioned to being an entrepreneur. I was self-employed. I was now the CEO. There were days I was living the American dream, and there were days I was living the American nightmare. That's the honest-to-God truth. However, in the end, I knew I'd done the right thing. I led (and still lead) a very rich life that had nothing to do with money. My life was not wrapped up in my identity as a real estate broker.

I was home every night with my family. I could go home for lunch because I lived five miles from my office. Just as I envisioned it, my children came up and played in my office. They had run of the whole building. I sat on the board of a couple of local charities. I never missed a school event. I was often the only dad at my daughters' school events. How do you put a price tag on that? How can someone look at that life and not recognize success?

If someone is making a million dollars a year and missing every school play, is that person really rich?

That's still what I do now as a speaker and author. But here is what I don't do. I don't stress out because I don't have some report complete for a boss who has depended on me to keep his own deadline. I don't have to hop in and out of airports and airplanes all week. I don't have to worry about offending someone with my convictions and beliefs and being overlooked for a promotion. I don't have to spend an average of 60 hours per week away from my family, and that's when I'm in town. Do I miss that? No!

That's not to say I didn't miss some aspects of corporate America after I made that move. We will get into that later when I give you the brutal truth about striking out on your own. I missed not having to pay the light bill. I missed not caring how much paper goes through the copier in a given day.

I missed some of my colleagues. I missed the "game" of making it in a big company. And sure, I even missed getting on an airplane once in a while if for nothing more than a change of scenery. I missed my nice paycheck that was never late and always cashed. I missed my medical insurance and my paid vacation. However, I'm still happy with my choice. What we are going to find out is whether or not you would be, too. Let's start by taking a look at your plan.

TIME TO GET REAL

1. If your life depended on your going to the moon, how would you do it? Seriously. Stop right now and list what your plan would be.
2. Write out your perfect day. What steps have you taken to create a life that allows this day? What steps do you still need to take?
3. What do you believe is your purpose on this earth? In what ways do you make sure you do at least one thing every day to manifest that purpose?

CHAPTER 3

PLANNING TO SUCCEED

"Success is simple. Do what's right, the right way, at the right time."
—ARNOLD H. GLASOW

Do you have a plan for your dream? I know it seems like such a "duh" question. However, I have to ask it. Do you have a plan? You cannot go into this world of self-employment without a well thought out plan. Well, I guess you could, but how dumb would that be?

Legendary football coach Vince Lombardi once said, "The desire to win is useless without the desire to prepare to win." So, be a pessimist for a moment. This can be tough because if you are real entrepreneur you are likely also a wide-eyed optimist. Regardless, you need to take a look at the absolute worst-case scenario. What will you do if you don't have one sale in your first six months? If you have no income for three months, how will you pay the mortgage?

Asking these tough questions is critical on a couple of levels. First, they get you to face the chance that you may fail. You need to get a sense of what that feels like in your gut. When I thought about it, it literally made me ill. That's because I'm always happier playing out these moments as hypothetical rather than in real life!

It's tempting to skip the planning part and move full-steam ahead following your enthusiasm to get things moving. However, I encourage you not to make this mistake. Do at least a five-year conservative proforma. If you can get through five years of your venture mentally, you will have a good plan in place. I survived more than five years, and I'm writing a book, so there must be something to it.

Also, look at how you will fund your retirement. Check into medical insurance costs. If it will require a move, buy your new house while you still have a current job. I just bought my first investment property as a business owner, and it was pretty easy. However, I know when it comes time to buy another house it will be trickier than when I had a verifiable job and income. When you are self-employed, you may find yourself not taking a paycheck for months on end. Plug all the gaps in your plan as best as you can. For instance, if you are going into a seasonal business, figure out how much money you will have to make during the peak seasons to get you through the downtimes. Once again, the critical thing is to be real with yourself. Be prepared for the moment your plan reveals something that makes you take a step back.

I remember when this happened to me. I realized that by buying my company under the initial financing terms, I would have no money in reserves to start out (all while being leveraged to the hilt). The solution? Three extra months of negotiation until the seller was willing to finance the company exactly how I wanted.

Another thing I encourage you to do is discuss your plan and your potential entrepreneurial venture with a trusted friend—preferably one with some business smarts. Encourage them to shoot holes in your plan. Be prepared to defend the plan. Don't get defensive (and assure the person that you won't do so). Let that person know he or she will be doing you an enormous disservice if he or she is not completely honest with you. Someone who can evaluate it objectively will assume a purely practical position, ignoring all the optimistic emotion that drives you. It's a good way to hear the questions you might not have asked yourself due to denial or possibly just oversight.

PLAY OUT ALL THE SCENARIOS

You need to visualize what it will look like if you hit the plan on all cylinders. What is your best-case scenario? Then you need to see what it looks like with a couple of hiccups. What if you only hit your gross profit by 70%? Can you still feed the family? Then there is scenario C. This is the toughest, but trust me, you will feel so much better having it in place. This is the scenario where you realize things just aren't working out as you planned—for whatever reason. It doesn't necessarily mean you have failed. It might just mean you weren't able to turn a profit or hire staff for your company as fast as you thought. Maybe your venture requires R&D that takes more time and money than you anticipated. Whatever the case, be prepared and decide right now what you will do if that day comes. The key to this plan is to reveal as many future realities as possible and have a strategy to deal with them. You don't want any surprises, although there will be some.

One of the biggest stress relievers of the whole process is coming up with the scenarios so that you have a plan if things go south. If you tell me you want to break out on your own, I might ask you, "What will you do if you don't sell one single gadget in the first year?" You can quickly reply, "Well, I'm going to cut advertising by 50%. I'm going to tap my credit line of..." You fill in the rest. The key is that you know what you're going to do if things don't pan out. What you will also realize is that you are going to live. It's going to be okay. If you're reading this book, you are most likely educated, even if that education came from the school of hard knocks. The men and women who pick up a book like this are not people who are going to find themselves holding a cup on a street corner. You're going to make it, even if you don't make it. You're in America. If you can't make it here, don't leave.

WRITE YOURSELF A LIFE PLAN

There are plenty of resources regarding how to write a good business plan. They are a dime a dozen. However, you also need to create a life plan. As Anthony de Mello so acutely said, "When you go through life with preferences but don't let your happiness depend on any one of them, then you're awake."

Ask yourself, "How much money do I actually need to be content?" In other words, how much money do you need to make every day to have your needs met? I guarantee it's not as much as you think. Now is a good time to do the math. List all your fixed costs such as utilities, mortgage or rent, automobile, food, and everything else you define as a life necessity. Once you get a monthly total multiply it by 12 and divide by 365. Once you get this number, calculate a daily amount. You will likely realize you can most likely live off much less than you think. Then start taking inventory of all the other "stuff" you spend money on. What could you abrogate from your life?

Ask yourself, "What really drives me? What do I want my life to look like day-to-day?" Go into this thing committing time to yourself and to your family. Personally, I messed up big time on this one when we moved to Tyler and I began my real estate business. I initially made no plans for days off or vacation. That left me with a seven-day-a-week schedule working 15 hours a day. Even though my office was practically in my neighborhood, it was as if I were still on the road because I was never home. I was also working Sundays, something I don't think God, the universe, natural law, family, or anything else blesses.

The closest thing I had planned for vacation was an international real estate convention, and it did not include my family. This poor decision caused major problems at home. My family was in a new town, a new house, under new circumstances, and I wasn't there. I was living at the office. Don't make this mistake. Commit to taking time off during that first year. You will be so glad you did.

I'll let you know upfront, taking time away as a business owner is not easy. Sadly, we've been programmed never to take time for ourselves. We aren't supposed to blow off an afternoon. Long vacations are for lazy Europeans, we say. You will start to believe that you are the only one who can keep the joint running. You will feel guilty for taking time away. You will start to be more concerned with your employees' image of you than your family's opinion if you aren't careful. Don't do that. Those aren't the reasons you set out to start living a life that you love.

I used to get so angry when someone might make a note of the fact I was going for a workout in the middle of the day. Finally, I realized it was my business. It was my time, and I couldn't care less what anyone thought of how I spent my time. Reading and meditating right in the middle of the day is perfectly fine. Just make sure you plan for time to reflect and plan. I'm not impressed with people who tell me they are "busy all the time." It tells me they can't plan their time efficiently.

Always remember why you made this decision to change your life. If you decided to strike out on your own, that's something to be proud of. Remind yourself of that. I can easily bog down in the daily rigors of entrepreneurship and forget just how lucky I am to do what I do. Therefore, take time to stop and observe your progress from an outsider's perspective. You'll be amazed at how motivating this can be. You'll move from thinking, "Why did I ever do this?" to thinking, "Wow, I want to make sure I keep this up." You won't want the ride to end, so plan time away from the shop. You will need it. It's healthy and it's definitely necessary. After all, you have given yourself freedom. So use it.

I'm speaking from experience and the lessons learned after I sold my business in 2013. I was burned out. I had acquired my company, lived the entrepreneur's dream, wrote a book about how great it was... and then completely burned out. I sold out, and let me tell you not a day goes by that I don't miss my real estate business. I want to be fully transparent with you. I executed my plan, and then in many ways took it for granted. Don't do that. If you gain momentum, hold onto it. That may mean you step away and recharge your batteries. Do whatever you have to in order to keep the engine burning. It's very difficult to start pushing that boulder again up the road.

I don't know what the magic number is, as far as time away. I'm sure there is some work-life balance book out there that tells exactly how much time off we need, but I haven't and don't plan to read it. The important thing to remember is that time off is recreation, as in re-creation. Nothing will make you more excited about what you're doing than stepping away and looking at it from a distance. There's just something about the daily marathon that mentally bogs you down. Therefore, plan for time out. If you are single, dedicate time to you. Travel, learn a new sport, and do something other than your routine. You didn't take on this risk and leave all that "security" to be burdened by work again.

If you are married with family, plan time that is devoted strictly to your spouse and kids. You will need your family now more than ever for support and trust. Many men reading this may have a wife who is very uneasy about taking this leap into business ownership. Show her you are planning time with her as part of this venture, and I guarantee she will be grateful. This simply must be a mutual decision because it's going to take a partnership.

I think one of the best aspects of having set out on my own is that if I had to go back and get a "real job" it would be a cakewalk. No more juggling the utility payments, the copier breaking down, or being an ad hoc network administrator. I could just go back to being a manager or whatever a company needed me to do. I always kept in mind that this could all come to an end someday. That's not because I wanted to cling to some doubt. It's because I want to remind myself that no matter what happens, I'm a much better businessperson as a result of this journey. You will be also. Therefore, you really can't fail...and if you do, you can at least be wiser for it.

If you truly think you're ready, start making the plan. Don't get in a hurry. By all means, don't rush this decision. I see now more than ever that there is no benefit to being hasty. Had I just waited a few months, I probably could have bought my company for 30% less than what I did. Just take your time. Set a date to implement your plan, but don't put artificial deadlines on yourself that are only going to cause you to stress if you don't reach them. The important thing is to start planning now. Make sure you have the time to get it all done. This means having time to prepare the family, the move, the money, everything. If you're ready, you will know it.

WHAT IS YOUR WHY?

I'm a fan of the movie *Sling Blade* about a slow-witted convict who killed his mother and was released into a halfway house program. The main character played by Billy Bob Thornton is named Carl. Upon his release, Carl gets a job at a small engine repair shop. One day the other workers, along with the owner of the shop, are vexed by their inability to get a lawnmower started. They have seemingly tried everything. Eventually, the owner calls Carl over. The first thing Carl does is kneel, remove the gas cap, and check to see if there is fuel present. He then looks up and says, "Ain't got no gas in it."

All that time, sweat and frustration could have been avoided had someone asked a very simple question. "Does it have gas in it?"

Precise, sometimes difficult and terribly thoughtful questions are vital. Asking "why" you want to do something different in your future is very powerful. Why is what sets the vision. "He who has a why to live can bear almost any how," Friedrich Nietzsche once said. What is it you want most from life and, more important, why do you want it? While there might be similarities in many cases, I think we all want a lot of money for a lot of different reasons. Why do you want to be free from your current job? Why do you want to take this huge risk of losing everything? This question is paramount. Once you find your why, your life will be more joyful and full of delight. There will be less confusion. You will better understand how all things are intertwined and working together and minimize feelings of dismay and bewilderment.

MY FIRST YEAR

I almost shudder when I replay my first year of entrepreneurship in my mind. I always had this big, empty feeling inside my stomach. I was constantly nervous. What if someone realized that I had no business running a real estate firm at the age of 28, having never sold a house in my life?

Learning what I was in for during year one won't add one thing to your venture, but I think you will find it a bit entertaining. Here I was, a young corporate schmuck who just up-and-decided one day to buy himself a little real estate firm. This wasn't just any real estate firm either. It was the oldest real estate company in Tyler. The average age of the agents was somewhere in the neighborhood of 60. The average tenure in this office was about 10 years. Who did I think I was? I was about to find out.

TIME TO GET REAL

1. What is your daily "burn" rate? How much money do you need to survive every day? If you haven't already done so, follow the instructions in this chapter to arrive at that number. What did this exercise teach you about how much money you actually need to be content?
2. Sketch out your life plan. Keep it simple. I don't care if you use colored pencils. Just make a list of what you want to do with the rest of your life. Start writing.
3. What is your why? See if you can condense your answer to one sentence.

CHAPTER 4

WHAT FREEDOM AFFORDS

"If I'm diagnosed with cancer, I won't seek treatment."
—JASON WRIGHT, FIRST YEAR OF SELF-EMPLOYMENT

I remember the first day I showed up at my new office. I randomly shook some hands as I passed people in the hall, but we didn't carry on too much as I had scheduled my introductory meeting for that afternoon. As I entered the conference room later, I noticed not one person was sitting at the table. Instead, everyone had lined the walls as though they were at an eighth-grade dance waiting to be asked. No one would make eye contact with me. My team looked old and bitter. As it turns out, most of them were exactly that. I just kept looking around the room and thinking, "My God, what have I done?"

I could see it in their faces. "Who does this rich little punk (whose mommy and daddy obviously bought him this place) think he is?" I knew that's what they were thinking. The good thing was that I was also smart enough to realize it didn't matter what they thought. I was on a mission, and they were either in or out. They didn't know that this was so much bigger than just buying a company and trying to scratch out a living. They were oblivious to my journey up to this point. They didn't know I'd gone through the planning, the agonizing self-doubt, and questioning. They just saw me as anyone else would have seen me. I was a young punk they didn't know, and I was coming in to shake up their world. They were also scared. Change was in the air. And changes scares the bejeebers out of people, especially those who are stuck in a rut.

Two minutes after I finished addressing the members of Misfit Island, one of the female agents immediately started asking me about the changes I planned to make.

Oh, she wasn't concerned with business, mind you. No, she had her mind on much more pressing issues, like what color I was going to paint the bathrooms. To this day, I don't think one of them ever asked me about myself and whether or not I needed any help. They just "wanted" from the beginning, and it was my job to "give."

In those early days, I ran on adrenaline most of the time. Like I said, I was in a constant state of nervousness for the better part of my waking hours. I was a stranger in my own company. I was not only learning on the job but also couldn't let anyone know just how little I actually knew about what I was doing. I had to demonstrate confidence and leadership. As I look back on those days, I know I was in God's hands. I couldn't have pulled it off alone. The cool thing is that when you are learning and running a business, you don't have time to stop and get down. It's as if you are riding this tidal wave, and you know you have to stay on top of it, or it will topple over you. That's what I did. I just kept going.

It took some time to get used to being not only a boss but also *the* boss. This still gets to me sometimes but in a good way. I have to stop and think when I get aggravated (and I do get aggravated) that I'm the guy. I'm the one people look to for guidance. For all the initial stress, my freedom afforded me some cool things, like the ability to do something I truly enjoy, which is to lead others. I like to inspire people to do more than they believe they are capable of doing. Looking back on this story, it's just another reminder that I am doing what I might not otherwise be able to do had I stayed in the rat race.

THE GOOD STUFF

Making the decision to take control of your life and start living out the things you are passionate about comes at a price. But freedom also affords you some rare opportunities. For example, I have always wanted to travel the other side of the world. I also have a desire to get outdoors. I love to hunt. I love the mountains. I love clean air and the lack of civilization. It's awesome. Figuring this passion into the equation of whether or not to go out on my own was a significant part of the decision.

As a matter of fact, it's a factor in why I'm writing and speaking today. I want to be free to hunt and hike and travel all over the world. I want to be able to speak to you at a conference on Monday and then head out to New Zealand on Wednesday for a Red Stag hunt. I also want to be able to live out my faith in a profound way. I'm sure you've figured out that I'm a Christian. I'm not going to beat that over your head. That's not what this book is about. That book will come later one day. I only mention my faith because it is foundation to one of the greatest experiences I've had to date.

In 2004, I went on my first-ever mission trip, hiking through the foothills of the Himalayas in the Hunan province of China. This was an unguided trip through some of the most remote areas on earth. It turned out to be life-changing, as I'll explain more in a later chapter.

More than once, I thought I was going to die. I had never pushed myself that far. However, I'm so glad I did it. It ties in perfectly with what I'm trying to convey to you. I knew this was a wild and scary trip I was signing on for, but I just did it anyway!

By throwing caution to the wind and acting on my passionate desire to serve God in a profound way, while also having a great adventure, I truly *lived* in that moment. Life is meant to be lived to the fullest. God intends for us to enjoy life. Why would he not? However, he's not going to pave the way. We have to look ourselves in the mirror and ask the person looking back, "What are you going to do to get the most out of this ride?" I think one of the best ways to do this is through our careers. It's where we all spend the majority of our waking hours. Wouldn't it make sense to do something we like?

This is part of the beauty of being out on your own. Yes, it involves a terribly large amount of risk, and it is hard, hard, work. However, you have the ability to shape your day, your week, and your month. You get to plan your work around a trip to China or wherever you wish to go. When I left corporate America, my calendar was suddenly filled with things like "Texas Day at Rylan's school" or "Christmas Pageant at Abby's school." These became the critical appointments I kept. One year, I was one of only two dads at my oldest daughter's Thanksgiving feast at school. Of all the things I have the freedom to do now, this might be the most profound. It's so gratifying to sit in the crowd, knowing one day—whether I'm rich or poor—my daughters will look back and remember Daddy was always there. Think for a moment of the safety and confidence that gives them.

If you're a dad, do you know what your true role is in this life? It's to be God. That's right. You are your kids' God. Now, if you do it right, you take your cues from our Father in Heaven and mimic as best as you can his actions and show your kids his love. Of course, in the early years your kids don't know the difference whether you are a great dad or not! You are their God anyway. It's critical to make this time to be there for them, to encourage them, and to cheer for them. They need to know their daddy is interested in their lives. I can't tell you how many times I've felt lumps in my throat out of my sincere gratitude for being able to witness some of these everyday school events with my kids.

DO YOU HAVE A RIGHT TO HAPPINESS?

I was standing at the gas station a few years ago filling up my Ford King Ranch F-250. It was black with tan trim. The signature King Ranch leather smelled like what I assume John Wayne's saddle must have smelled like. It was four-wheel drive and, in a word, beautiful. I had wanted a King Ranch for some time. I had no business owning one because this truck was designed to pull a heavy payload. All I carried were my daughters on occasion. They didn't take up all that much room, and I never got paid for carrying them.

I've yet to encounter a muddy street in my city to date, but should one have popped up, I was prepared. Diesel engine? Check. And I needed all the power I could muster while cruising the roads of East Texas. This truck was nothing but a huge vanity purchase. I was bored and had a little money, so I bought my dream truck. However, that's my business. It was a stupid purchase. It was a wasteful purchase, but it was my business. I had earned the right through hard work to drive such an impractical vehicle. I had worked my tail off, saved the money, and she was mine.

That day at the gas station, someone pulled up beside me pulled up a different car. It was a beat-up domestic ride of some kind. I can't remember the exact make. Out hopped a young man of around 16. He looked at my truck and immediately commented on how nice it was. He then proceeded to give me a sob story about his car. "I have to drive this car," he moaned. "I just hope it will keep running. I would love to have a truck like yours, but this is all I can afford."

Since you weren't there that day, you will have to trust me this wasn't just a teenager admiring my truck. He was truly begging for sympathy about his poor ride. Instead of feeling sorry for him, I wanted to cut across to his side of the pumps and ask him why he was even suggesting at his age he should be driving a truck such as mine. What gave him any idea he deserved such a truck? I left the station stunned to a certain degree. The longer I thought about it, the angrier I became. I actually felt guilty for a moment at the pump. It wasn't until I later processed his words I became aware of his frame of mind.

This young guy doesn't just represent his millennial generation either. He represents much of America at any age these days. We've been sold this false bill of goods that we "deserve" happiness. Since when do we deserve happiness? Who made this stupid claim for the first time? Can someone please substantiate this claim? You can't. It's not in the Bible. It's not in the Koran. It's not even in the Constitution. The Constitution does guarantee us the right to pursue happiness. It does not say we have the right to happiness.

Whatever life you are seeking, if you want to taste the fruits of meaningfulness and success, you are most likely going to have to work your posterior off. It's that simple. Oh, and after all the hard work, the sweat, the tears, and the pain, you may not find success or happiness. Nothing is guaranteed. However, we do know what Ray Kroc, the man responsible for making McDonald's a household name, said is true. "Luck is a dividend of sweat. The more you sweat, the luckier you get." There simply isn't any substitute for hard work. You do not deserve happiness. You only deserve the right to pursue it. More on this in a later chapter where I'll teach you the difference between joy and happiness.

I heard a story about a young man who was a basketball player. He had been invited to a competition of premier Hoosiers. After practice, he asked the coach if there was a way to get a ride home later so he could stay and put in some more work. The coach said he would arrange a ride back to the hotel later that day.

The player stayed and took hundreds of extra shots. He went to every spot he was likely to find himself shooting in a game and took shot, after shot, after shot. Eventually, after hours of extra shooting and working up a sweat, he decided to call it a day. The tournament happened to be the U.S. Olympics where the American "Dream Team" premiered. The player was Larry Bird. Stop and think about that for a moment. If Larry Bird, one of the single greatest players to ever take the court, was willing to stay and put in hours of extra work and extra sweat, what gives any of us the right to believe we deserve success unless we're willing to do the same thing? Larry Bird realized the more sweat he put in during practice, the luckier he became on the court in a game.

You have to work and work hard. Another example is Don Mattingly. Growing up I thought the New York Yankees star Don Mattingly had one of the sweetest swings in baseball. I loved watching "Donny Baseball," even though I was an Atlanta Braves fan. Mattingly was at that time one of the best contact hitters in the game. As gifted as he was, he would arrive at the stadium early every day and take 500 swings off the tee before regular batting practice started.

I wanted to include a story of someone I knew who had worked tirelessly and yet had not achieved success. I intended to use it as an example of the fact that there are no guarantees. However, I couldn't think of one. Why? It's because we don't hear about quitters. We don't hear about those who stop short of achieving their goals. There are few people like The Colonel, Harland Sanders, of KFC fame who tried and failed over and over and over until they finally made it. Sanders actually slept in his car at one point, driving around trying to get people to buy his recipe for fried chicken.

At 45 years old, Zig Ziglar was dead broke. However, he still got up before dawn and would go to a Rotary Club or manufacturing facility to speak. He was determined to be a success. Michael Jordan didn't even make his high school basketball team at first. However, he kept honing his skills until he developed into the greatest basketball player of all time. He didn't deserve to be the greatest; he only had the right to pursue being the greatest, and that's exactly what he did.

This truth isn't new. It's just not. However, we humans need to hear a truth repeatedly until one day it sticks. I think truisms like these are like a shower. You can never take a shower once and be clean forever. Just because you've heard a great song once doesn't mean you won't enjoy it again. In fact, when we hear a favorite song that we haven't heard in years, we often remember how beautiful it really is. That's what these lessons are. They are timeless. They are a hit song that pays royalties forever, because they ring true.

Persistence is key. Do you want to be happy? No, I mean it. Do you REALLY want to be happy? Okay, so the answer is "yes." Fine. What are you willing to do to get there? How many times will you suffer unhappiness to get to happiness? As with any other worthwhile pursuit, you must be persistent in your pursuit of happiness. You must determine you will not stop until you can sit back and whisper, "Life is beautiful."

Napoleon Hill in his classic book *How to Think and Grow Rich* says, "Those who have cultivated the habit of persistence seem to enjoy insurance against failure. No matter how many times they are defeated, they finally arrive up toward the top of the ladder." Read Hill's words again carefully. I have learned in my 43 years that I am the only one who can decide when the fight is finished and the pursuit is over. No one else will ever tell me I'm defeated. Life is a game, and we are allowed to adjust the rules to suit our needs. If you punch me in the face, I have a choice. I can either be furious and punch you back, or I can absorb the punch and turn it into a stoic lesson on emotional control.

If I lost all my speaking and writing gigs tomorrow, I could panic and fret and consider going broke. I would not have a way to pay for Abby's diabetes medication, and I would dread having to tell my wife of less than one year that I'm broke and unemployed. Or I can decide this is only the 43rd of my 80 plus years on this earth, so I have plenty of time to strategize this thing out. It might be painful in the near term, but I know one day it will end. Whatever dreams I have of writing, speaking, and encouraging others will not be shattered simply because life has thrown me a curve.

I know what it's like to live in a pretty defeated state. Many of the things I wrote about in my first book are gone. However, I'm still here. There is still more life to live, experiments to try, businesses to pursue, victories to be had, and goals to be achieved. The key is to persist. We must be patient. When you have a goal before you and think of life as a game, the journey and the ups and downs become part of it.

Fill in the blank on the following sentences:
- I will quit my dream if...
- My happiness is not worth full persistence because...
- I could work as hard as Larry Bird, but I won't because...

I hope if you thought of the answers to any of these questions you immoderately punched yourself in the face! Don't give up!

WHEN TO PUSH THE BUTTON

One of the things that frustrated me the most about working for the other guy was that every other Friday I knew exactly how much my pay would be. I couldn't do anything to increase that paycheck from one week to the next. It was what it was, and that was it. I couldn't use my God-given business sense and creativity to create true wealth the way I wanted to do it. I just showed up, and the company paid me. I was contributing to someone else's dream.

Now it's different. Again, these are things you can't put a price tag on, but they are the things in life that ultimately matter. This is living. Living out my dream has given me the ability to take advantage of these times. But when is it the right time to push the button?

TIME TO GET REAL

1. If you acted on your dreams, what are the top three benefits you stand to gain?
2. What would you change if you had the unrestricted ability to shape your day, your week, and your month?
3. How hard are you working on your dreams now? At maximum capacity? Occasionally? What more do you need to do?

CHAPTER 5

WHY NOT YOU?

"...for we are his workmanship."
—EPHESIANS 2:10

When I published my book in 2010, the United States was in the worst recession in decades. We were reaching staggering unemployment numbers, the likes of which we hadn't seen in my lifetime. People were losing homes, businesses were closing, banks were failing, and there was an overall fear in our country that we couldn't seem to shake.

Logically speaking, these circumstances were enough to make anyone do whatever they could to keep their job and not take any unnecessary risks. Logically speaking, it would have been crazy to leave a job when so many couldn't even find one, right? But I knew our country was ready even in the midst of the recession to embrace a new sort of entrepreneur more than ever. There were fewer reasons for people to operate the way they once did. This was the age of the "independent consultant."

By the close of the 20th century, the U.S. was back and at record low unemployment. It turns out I was right. More and more people are thriving in the service economy. Jobs are being created that didn't even exist a year ago. By the time my daughters finish college, the jobs that existed when they entered college will no longer be around, while jobs that didn't exist when they entered will be created. It's truly an amazing time to be alive.

Don't underestimate this curious little hindrance called "logic." It will be the first roadblock you encounter when you step up to the plate to take a swing at your dream. Logic is a very useful tool—until it morphs into fear. Logic will tell you, "There is no way you can do that." Logic will say, "This is not the time to be chasing some wild dream of yours." Both of these statements may very well be true, logically speaking. For instance, if you cannot leave your current job because by staying through the end of the year you are guaranteed a $10,000 bonus, I'd say it's worth staying! That would be logical. However, if you are not stepping out because you don't think you have the skillset and talent, that is fear.

Let's work through this a bit. At the end of this chapter, it will be up to you to decide the difference between logic and fear as it applies in your situation. I'm just going to help you think through it. If you still don't have an inkling on when you want to step out, then I suggest you devote yourself to some serious prayer and lots of alone time to process it completely. No one can choose for you. It's all on you to decide.

YOU ARE YOUR GREATEST ASSET

Let's say you recently lost your job. Maybe that's why you picked up this obscure little book. To you I say, "Breathe easy." It's going to be okay. How do I know? Well, in a way, I'm in a similar situation. My core business during the recession was real estate. Unless you've been under a rock lately, you know real estate was a tough business in 2010. Granted, I lived in a part of the country that wasn't hit like many others, but I harbored a lot of anxiety, nevertheless. However, I can tell you this economic downturn turned out to be one of my biggest motivators. I got into the "Jason Wright" business more than ever before. I got busy hedging my bets and adding as much value to my greatest asset—me. You are your greatest asset. What are you doing to use this time of unemployment to learn, read, write, and do something to develop as a person? I'll give you a specific plan in another chapter, so stay tuned, but chew on that thought for now.

I can almost guarantee there is work out there for you. There may not be a job per se, but there is work. What is your trade? Are you a network administrator, for example? I can tell you firsthand that small businesses who can't afford to employ a full-time administrator always need someone to call when a router goes down, or a PC is just acting weird. Give your name to these businesses. You may find one day you have to add an employee to take all the calls! Before you know it, the company who laid you off may be losing business to yours.

At the risk of oversimplifying what may or may not happen in your situation, I want you to focus on the possibilities. Just because you don't have a job doesn't mean there is no work. There is always going to be work to do in America. The question is if you're going to be the one to go find it and build a business around it.

Independent entrepreneurs are popping up everywhere. For instance, take Stacey Kannenberg, who built an entire business around being a mom. Stacey is an author, publisher, speaker, motivator, consultant, blogger, spokesperson, and Mom CEO for children's education issues and what she calls "Mom Entrepreneurship." Her books have sold over 60,000 copies and are used inside over 400 school districts nationwide. She specializes in viral marketing to brands, businesses, authors, and publishers.

Impressive stuff, but Stacey is just like you and me. She had a dream, drive, and will to pursue it—and boom, she's living the American dream. Stacey also knows everything there is to know about self-promotion, and there has never been a better time to do this in America (or anywhere for that matter). Facebook, LinkedIn, Instagram, Vimeo, Wordpress, Twitter, and any number of other social networking sites put you in control of promoting yourself. Thanks to technology, you no longer have to beg, plead, and pray for some publisher, or agent, or guru will take you in and decide they can make enough money off you to help you in your work. Instead, you can be your own publisher and publicist.

Let's take my unemployed network administrator a step further in his new world as an independent consultant. If he's like the millions of others on social media, the day he was laid off from ABC, Inc. he probably posted a sad status notification saying that he was now out of a job. Followed by the plea for anyone who knew of any openings anywhere to please give him a call. Instead, he could have posted the following:

"Excited to announce I've started my own Network Administration Practice. If you are a small business in need of big solutions, please call me."

If he's like me, he has nearly 600 friends who would see his post, including some small business owners. Next, he could create a Facebook page for his new business separate from his personal page. He could invite people to become fans. In addition, he could start a blog where he posts links to his Facebook page. He could then start a Twitter page where he announces his blog updates and notes about heading out to client sites. Here's the really exciting part of this example. The total cost for this word-of-mouth marketing campaign is $0.

Nothing will force you to do something out of the ordinary like a catastrophe. There's something about the whole "nothing to lose" mentality that will generate some of the peak potential in all of us. If you are in one of those moments, swat the fear away and capitalize on the opportunities. The media's take on the economy, political scene, your current job, or anything else might be telling you now is not the time to jump out on your own. But if you look at it from a different perspective, you may find there has never been a better time to go for it.

TRADE IN YOUR EXCUSES

Imagine you were in my office right now discussing your dream for your life. If I said, "Tell me why you can't do this?" what would you say? My guess is you might say something along the lines of the following: "I'm not smart enough" or "I'm not a risk-taker" or "I don't know enough people" or "I don't have enough money" or even "I just don't see myself being someone who can do that sort of thing." Well, let's get into who you are.

First, there is the spiritual component of who you are. If you are not a believer in God, or his Son, Jesus Christ, please give me a little grace here. I will address you, too. However, for me to write a chapter about "who we are" and not mention God would be like describing the fastest car ever made and never once mentioning the designer. It would be ridiculous.

With that said, who does God say you are? The Bible states in Ephesians Chapter 2, we are "God's workmanship." We are a walking, talking illustration of the skill of the Creator of the universe. God made it all, but we are his true masterpiece. Van Gogh could have made a peanut butter and jelly sandwich, and it might have been good, but his masterpiece was not sandwich-making. It was *Sunflowers* or any of the other paintings that showed his true skill.

Of all the things God has created, we are his greatest design. If we are his workmanship, and we are created in the image of God Almighty, I'd say we have some pretty amazing talents. You have to believe this, or it won't make a difference in your life. Jesus told his disciples, "For truly I say to you, if you have faith like a grain of mustard seed, you will say to this mountain, 'Move from here to there,' and it will move, and nothing will be impossible for you," (Matthew 17:20). I realize my faith is small at times, but for those who believe and desire God to be glorified through them, that's all it takes for him to do amazing things.

If you don't have faith in what you're doing, you're toast. You simply must have faith in your decision at this point. Hope is one thing. Faith is conviction and it's an entirely different matter. Hope says, "It will be great if this works out." Faith says, "I believe it will." You simply cannot transition to a greater life, an entrepreneurial venture, or anything of any real consequence without great, big faith.

It's faith that keeps you going when everything around you says not only that it can't be done, but also you're a fool for even entertaining such a thought. Here's what is likely to happen when you dive off into the big black abyss of uncertainty. Your subconscious will necessarily come in conflict with your actions. That's because we have auto-neuro sensors that tell us when we are up to something that could lead to chaos or harm.

You know by now that I am a very big fan of Tony Robbins. Much of what I discuss in this chapter, I learned from him about neuro-associations. A simple neuro-association goes like this: I think of raking the leaves and I imagine misery. I think of eating bananas foster and I think of bliss. We have a neuro-association with everything that either equals pleasure or pain. I learned from Tony you can actually disrupt these patterns. You can train yourself to have the neuro-association you desire.

Our brains function in a very literal and objective manner. For instance, think of your car right now. If you suddenly received a phone call that you had to be somewhere nearby because Rob Base and DJ EZ Rock were about to give a live performance of "It Takes Two," your brain would be at ease. The default neuro alert would inform you that you could get there and take in this spectacle. You wouldn't even have to conjure up faith in the fact that your car would start. That's because every time you get in the car, it starts. No faith required. Your brain has been trained by this outcome happening over and over.

So, following this logic, what you have to do is exercise faith continuously. Every time doubt creeps in, try shouting, "Stop!" Then proceed to tell yourself that you know without a doubt you will reach the outcome you desire. Tell yourself you have faith that your desired outcome will show itself because you have faith in your pursuit. Do this repeatedly, and eventually, the auto-neuro sensor of faith will trigger.

Faith is not just a Christian thing either. Every major religion or spiritual belief teaches the importance of faith. One of the paramount reasons you must have faith during any meaningful endeavor is the fact that you're taking a huge risk. Great risk and comfort seldom make good bedfellows. To the contrary, risk brings on uncertainty, which we are not conditioned as humans to find comfort in.

I use this tactic to increase my faith. I train myself to respond to any fear or doubt with the sentence, "I have enormous faith." For example, I do this every time I start to doubt the publication of this book or the thought of making my living as a speaker and author.

A friend of mine recently introduced me to Jon Acuff after I explained to him how I thought it was time to do what I knew I was called to do all along: write and speak.

My friend was very encouraging and told me I needed to look at some of Jon's work. I did, and immediately my mind associated doubt with the existence of Jon Acuff. I watched Jon speak, looked at his books, and thought, "Oh crap. There's already a "me" out there! The world doesn't need me. It has Jon Acuff!" I gave a man who is terribly talented and pretty much living my dream credit for having cornered the entire market of speaking and writing. As though there was no room for anyone else!

I immediately realized what I was doing and knew I had to find a way to train my brain to respond differently. Instead of getting down and thinking I could never achieve what Jon has, I started saying to myself, "I have enormous faith that the world needs me to speak when Jon Acuff isn't available." I trained myself to look at Jon as confirmation of the need for my work, instead of thinking there was no work left for another speaker like me to do.

When faith becomes your auto-response, you immediately have peace. You cut yourself so many breaks. You're able to tell yourself you don't have to have it all figured out right now. You don't have to get the book finished right away. You don't have to raise all the capital at once. Faith tells you there's another way to get this done that you haven't even seen, so just be patient. This principle is so very powerful. Having faith relieves my burdens, and it may be the single most powerful element of all for me.

I tend to let obstacles in my mind build up until they have secured a vast walled vault around my dream. If I let this go on long enough, the walls will be so high and so fortified that my dream ceases to exist. In the worst-case scenario, the vault gets sealed and my dream completely dies for lack of oxygen. However, exercising my faith keeps the walls from going up. It keeps my dream visible. It's that mental check that says, "Dude, chill out! This is a journey. This isn't a jigsaw puzzle. All the pieces haven't been formed yet, but they will be."

The concept of enjoying the journey is something I have forever struggled with. I want what I want, and I want it now. I don't want to wait. I don't like to wait. Impatience has been a devastating weakness for me for years. I harken back to Gary Vaynerchuk saying over and over to enjoy the journey and practice patience.

TAKE A LOOK BACK

I think it's helpful to look back on occasion to see the evidence of your faith confirmed. I guarantee you there have been times in your life you thought there was no way "something" was going to happen, and it did. Stop right now and picture that time. Think back to all the fretting and worry before the thing came through.

I'm not talking about a random, out of the blue event. I'm talking about a time when you didn't think you were going to be able to bear children, and now you have a beautiful daughter. I'm talking about the time you didn't think there was any way you would get that job, and you applied anyway and got it. Just look back on the moments in your life where all the data presented showed that your dream shouldn't work out, but you just knew it would. You put one step in front of the other toward that outcome, and it worked out. The reason why I asked you to recall this situation is because it's always easier to believe something will happen again, than to believe it will happen the very first time.

Most of our worst fears rarely, if ever, come true. I know many of you who have a burn in your gut for something you desperately want to do, but you are avoiding acting on it because of fear. Ask yourself, "What's the worst that could happen?" The worst-case scenario is not going to kill you. But here's the good news. Odds are, it's not going to happen at all.

That's one thing my 40-plus years on this earth have taught me. Most of the stuff I worried myself sick over never happened. However, some did happen, and I am a better man having walked through those fires. None of it killed, injured, or paralyzed me. They made me better. I am not one to ever suggest blind faith and or irrational behavior. I'm just telling you to sharpen and nurture your faith. It's so very powerful and necessary to make a significant life change.

Now I suggest you pop in some Rob Base and DJ EZ Rock and challenge someone to a breakdance battle. It will not strengthen your faith. It will not change your life. It will, however, be awesome because, after all, it's Rob Base and DJ EZ Rock.

LOOK AT YOUR CAPABILITIES

For the non-believer, I have only common sense to offer you. There is nothing more intelligently designed than the human being. No computer can compute as fast as the human brain. No animal walking the earth has more intellect, skill, logical reasoning, or abilities than that of the human. We are at the tip-top of the food chain. I challenge you to step back and objectively look at the skills you have. Realize how truly amazing we are and the potential we all possess, and you will begin to grasp what you are capable of doing.

I was at a high school football game one Friday and noticed a surgeon in the crowd. He's known around town for being a much-respected physician, as well as an incredibly wealthy guy. As I looked at him, it occurred to me, "He's a man. I'm a man. He's just reached his full potential." We all have the ability to reach our peak performance. Do we all have the ability to be surgeons? No, not any more than we all have the ability to hit a 90mph fastball. And yet, there is something in us that is only in us!

Coach Lombardi also said, "The human body is the most amazing of all machines in that it can endure almost anything." All humans are incredible beings. It is a human who splits the atom. It is a human who carries a football. It is a human who performs open-heart surgery. It was a human who wrote every piece of music ever known. There are so many things we are all capable of, no matter who we are or what season of life we find ourselves in. Get your mind around just how special, complex, and perfectly designed you are and do something with it.

NOW OR LATER?

Hopefully, I've convinced you by now that you can do it. But when should you do it? That's the question. You still may be unsure if this is the right time to make a change in your life. The simple fact is there is no magic bullet. However, there are some prominent factors at play.

First, time isn't standing still. If you continue waiting for the perfect moment to arrive, you will be waiting from now on. Tim Ferriss wrote in *The 4-Hour Workweek*, "I once asked my mom how she decided when to have her first child, little ol' me. The answer was simple: 'It was something we wanted, and we decided there was no point in putting it off.' The timing is never right to have a baby." Going out on your own or trying to realize any dream is like deciding to have a child. There will never be a perfect time. There will always be a reason to put it off until next year when things will be a little better. Money is always going to be a factor. If you had enough money (acknowledging "enough" is a relative term), chances are you might not ever step out. After all, you would have enough money to do nothing! Having enough money may very well end up being your trap. Not having all the money you need to make your move may actually be your best motivator. Like going on a diet or deciding to exercise, it's always best to start tomorrow or next week.

I remember a guy I worked with had a little sign on his desk that read, "Do it now." I'm not suggesting you become haphazard in your actions. That would be completely counter to my core beliefs about planning. But what are you waiting for? You're not getting any younger, I assure you. Whatever roadblocks you may have now will only be replaced by others later. I don't mean for you to throw down this book and go type up your resignation letter. That would be silly. However, you can start planning now. You can start asking the right questions now and building enthusiasm for whatever is next in your life.

As I mentioned earlier, I once lived under self-inflicted timelines that did nothing but make me miserable. One of the reasons I jumped out on my own so young was the feeling that time was just a-wastin'. Every day that slipped by seemed one less day to pursue my goals. Early on, I sometimes thought I might have jumped too soon. Looking back, however, I'm so glad I just sacked up and went for it.

Do it now, but dream it now, too. I'm a man living out the American dream, and yet I continue to dream. This isn't to say I'm not happy where I am, or that I am looking for something different. I just like to imagine what God might have in store for my family and me in the future. Don't be afraid to imagine what it would be like if your dreams come true. It's not going to happen by buying some late-night infomercial kit on how to place classified ads. It's going to happen by planning and reminding yourself of your dream frequently.

Simply setting aside time to ponder the potential of your dream is doing something. Just get moving. If you are seriously considering stepping out on your own, then get ready—a tremendous change is on its way.

TIME TO GET REAL

1. Which one is driving most of your decisions related to your dreams—logic or fear? Why is that? How can you get both to work in your favor instead?
2. What do you need to do that you've been putting off? What action step can you take this week toward accomplishing this goal?
3. In what ways are you exercising faith in yourself and your dream on a regular basis?

CHAPTER 6

CHANGE: WHAT A SCARY THING

"Things do not change; we change."
—HENRY DAVID THOREAU

How often do we do things we hate (or what we know is bad for us) just because of our defiant refusal to change? We eat too much because we don't like the idea of switching to a healthier diet. We don't exercise because we don't want to change our schedule to include the necessary work exercise presents. We'll even stay in a job we hate because we fear the unknown. We know we hate the job...but at least we know the job we hate!

You've likely seen the tragic scenes that television news helicopter crews capture during hurricane season every year. In some cases, dozens of people sit stranded on top of their roofs amid litter-filled, murky water. Whenever I see this footage, I can't believe so many of the victims refused to get out of harm's way when there was adequate time to evacuate. They stay in (or in many instances "on") their homes. For some, leaving their house behind (despite the warnings) was never an option. I understand that. But I can't understand risking your life to stay simply because the idea of making a drastic change is frightening. Refusing to leave behind the life they know left them sitting and staying in a watery hell.

The thought of leaving behind your whole world as you know it may be just as frightening as being caught in a hurricane. However, with any change, there is a silver lining—a new life just waiting for you to explore. You only have to choose whether or not to embrace it.

WAKE UP TO CHANGE

Personally, I hate change. I love routine, and I crave predictability. One of the most difficult considerations for me about moving to Tyler to do the real estate business was the huge change in my routine. I wouldn't have my same Kroger to shop. I wouldn't have my usual gas station. I wouldn't even have my beloved Mr. Car Wash that I used to go to on Saturdays. However, I knew I would be able to start new routines and carve out a new way of doing things. Guess what? I did. I often knew exactly what I was going to do and where I was going to be on any given day.

I firmly believe a routine, however, can ultimately become a rut, and that's nowhere you need to be. Have you ever noticed people who work out so hard in the gym and yet never seem to change their appearance? I used to go up to my local gym early every morning to work out. This guy (who shall remain nameless) was always there sweating, grunting, and working out with amazing intensity.

However, I noticed something as time went on. His physical appearance never looked any different. He never seemed to lose weight or gain muscle definition. I used to think to myself how frustrating this must be for the guy. Eventually, I figured out what was going on. He was doing the same exercises every time he worked out. While I'm sure there was some benefit to this, he wasn't changing his body composition. Why? Because his muscles had learned his routine and turned it into a rut. His muscles knew what to expect every day, and therefore, they stopped growing.

If we want to grow spiritually, mentally, or physically, we need to change our routine. Our behavior must change. I have grown so much as a leader, business thinker, money manager, father, and husband since I stepped out on my own. It allowed me to mature in ways I never thought possible. There are many times when I look back on the jobs I've had and start to beat myself up for leaving some of them. However, I would never be the businessman I am today had I stayed. I wouldn't have a reason or the credibility to write or speak on issues. I would just be a staffer trying to keep up with the game. Thank God I didn't stay. Instead, I built a collage of experiences, and these let me become more than I was.

CHANGE MEANS PRUNING

"Do something that scares you every day," wrote Eleanor Roosevelt. When I changed my career, city of residence, and industry years ago, it was stressful and scary as all get out. It really was. However, my goal outweighed any discomfort this drastic change in my life presented. It held my focus. That's why it's so critical to have an end game in mind. When you feel fear creep into the pit of your stomach, remind yourself why you are making a change.

Change will make you grow in ways you never thought possible. Like flowers, we need pruning to grow to our fullest. A flower will be pretty for a while, but then the bloom will shrivel, lose its color, and appear dead. But if you pluck or prune the old head of the flower, a new and often prettier and larger one will replace it. We need to be willing to prune ourselves in order to stimulate growth. That might mean cutting off old habits. It might mean cutting ourselves off from a dead end job. Only you know what it is that you need to cut away in order to grow a fuller and more prosperous life.

Do you ever look at the beggar on the street and think for a moment that he is someone's child? He was once a newborn baby with a full life ahead of him, only to find himself holding a sign begging for money on the street corner. How does that happen? I once knew a man who was jobless and homeless. When I first came across his story, I discovered he'd once fallen asleep on a sidewalk in the rain outside a pawn shop in soiled clothes. That's right. He had gotten so low that he didn't even find a bathroom when it came time to relieve himself. He was even considering suicide.

By all accounts, he had once been a normal person. He didn't come from an abusive home. His mother was encouraging to him as a child, often telling him how he would one day become a great writer. His father was a hard worker who provided for his family. The young boy grew up and soon became a pilot in World War II. He even flew with the actor and war hero Jimmy Stewart on some thirty combat missions.

However, due to poor life choices, the man lost everything. He lost his wife, his precious daughter, and his home. What followed was his dignity, his pride, and everything that had once made him a "normal" person. The gentleman's name is OG Mandino. Many of you may have heard of OG. He was a best-selling author of such books as *The Greatest Salesman in the World* and *A Better Way to Live*. I look up to OG, although I have never actually met him in person, only through his writings.

In his book *A Better Way to Live*, he writes about his past:

"Sadly, I'm afraid, that same scenario is repeated hundreds of times every day in this beautiful country of ours when people finally lose their last shred of hope in a tomorrow that once held so much promise. And that doesn't count the thousands who don't take their lives but give up anyway. They quit on themselves. They let all their dreams fade into the twilight. They stop trying and just exist, leading what Thoreau called 'lives of quiet desperation.' They're already dead, at age twenty-five or thirty or forty or even fifty, for all they're accomplishing…even though we won't be burying them until they're seventy-two."

OG Mandino went from being a homeless, alcoholic bum to a world-renowned speaker and author. How? Because he realized when he was about to throw his life away just how precious life is. It's a good thing, too, because countless lives have changed as a result of his teaching and writing.

CHANGE CAN BE GOOD

The residents of New Orleans didn't have a choice in the aftermath of Katrina's devastation. They had to change their lives and relocate to a new home. If you're employed, how fortunate you are right now to have a choice. You aren't being forced into anything. I remember a lot of would-be-agents interviewed with me after a life-changing event. One woman was in her mid-40s, with no wedding ring and no résumé. I soon discovered she had two kids, was recently divorced and now, to add to her already stressful life, she wanted to get into a commission-only job, one of the most difficult arenas to be successful in early on in your career. On the other hand, I admired her guts. She went through the not-so-easy process of getting her real estate license (which means taking a tough test that adults hate). She endured some of the most tedious and boring classes known to man, and now she was in my office looking for a second chance in life.

I know a woman whose story is very similar, save for the divorce. When she married her husband, they both brought children to the new marriage. For the first few years, they struggled. He was a truck driver, and she stayed at home. After a couple of years, the husband opened a tire store, and she kept the books. As a team, they worked the business very well and grew a solidified company with substantial annual revenues and a great market share.

However, as is the case with many husband-and-wife business owners, they started to see their share of troubles. He did business one way; she did it another. Their disagreements caused friction, and she eventually decided she'd had enough of the tire business and bookkeeping. At the suggestion of a friend, she started taking real estate classes and pursued her real estate license. Her children were reaching college age, and she had more time to invest in a new venture. Now, you have to understand something. She was a woman who had never sold anything in her life. She just wanted something that was hers. She wanted a change. She wanted something that was her achievement. Was she scared? I think so. Was she confident in her abilities? I think not. However, she forged ahead.

After nine months in real estate, she was a multi-million dollar agent. She was also going head-to-head with the other top dog in the office. She soon became far and away the top salesperson in the office and even earned the top national honor for her franchise. The once tire store bookkeeper now owns her own office. As a matter of fact, she owns five offices. She reached the pinnacle of success as an agent, and hers is now one of the top franchises in the entire system. Other industry experts look to her for advice and guidance.

I know this story pretty well because the woman who achieved this is my step-mother. I watched my mom go from housewife, to bookkeeper, to entrepreneur, and it has been an awesome and inspiring sight to behold. My step-mother grew up in Saltillo, Texas, with no business training whatsoever. But she had a dream and got fed up with her "status quo" life. So what did she do? She changed. She got out of her comfort zone and started living the American dream. I'm really proud of and for her.

My step-mother suffered an aneurysm in 2019. By all accounts she shouldn't be alive. However, her grit and determination have sustained her, and her business has grown exponentially. She is truly an amazing woman and business leader, and I could not be more proud of her.

UNEXPECTED CHANGE

It was February 7, 2017. I received a call and learned our youngest daughter, Abby, who was 16 at the time was having some issues. She was feeling weak and sick. The morning began with Abby upstairs in the bathroom thinking she may throw up. Abby had not been feeling well for some time. She had dozed off in class, had a huge appetite yet, was losing weight to the tune of 15 pounds in less than three weeks.

After receiving Abby's bloodwork, our family physician told us we needed to get Abby to the emergency room at once. Her blood sugar levels were at 400. It was then that I learned what Type 1 diabetes is. Of course, I had always heard of diabetes. I thought it had something to do with people eating too much sugar or something. It was one of those distant health problems that happened to "other" people. Now we were faced with it happening in our family.

Abby would be flown by helicopter to Dallas Children's Hospital. It was almost a certainty she had diabetes, the doctors in our local emergency room told me. I was numb. There is nothing worse than hearing your little girl has a problem you cannot fix. Her sister, Rylan, and I drove to Dallas. Rylan is extremely close to her little sister, who is only 15 months younger than her, and she was worried sick. I had to maintain my composure for her sake, when all I wanted to do was break down and cry.

This day started out like any other. However, our lives changed forever. Type 1 diabetes is a life-threatening and life-altering disease for which there is no cure. Abby will forever be calculating carbs, pricking her finger, and praying she never finds herself without insulin when needed. Her purse is no longer an accessory but a carrier of life-saving meds. To this day, Abby has not complained. She doesn't let diabetes stop her from being who she is. She ran track, became an amazing cook, and is, in a word, my hero.

Some of you have endured far worse. You've heard the word, "leukemia." You've heard the phrase, "congestive heart failure." None of us is immune to the many curves life can throw us. Disease and tragedy remind us how frail life is.

WE SHARE A UNIVERSAL DIAGNOSIS

Actor Michael Landon, who died of cancer, once said, "Somebody should tell us right at the start of our lives that we're dying and we might live life to the limit. Every minute of every day. Do what I say. Whatever you do, do it now. There are only so many tomorrows."

Well, it's not the beginning of your life, but here I am—telling you. I'm not a doctor nor do I play one on TV, but I'm here with a diagnosis. I don't need a medical degree to give you absolute certainty that my diagnosis is 100 percent accurate. You can get a second opinion, and I will still guarantee you I'm right. Here is the diagnosis: you're dying. Yes, you. You are dying. There is nothing I or anyone else can do to save you. I'm sorry.

You may feel well right now, but rest assured you are dying, and there's nothing you can do to stop it. There is no punchline coming to tell you this is just hypothetical. It's real. Unfortunately, I share the same diagnosis. We all do. Regardless of what you believe about Heaven or hell, we're dying and on the way out. Will it be five years from now or five minutes? We have absolutely no way of knowing for sure.

The Greek philosophers referred to this mindset as *momento mori,* *meaning* "You must die." This truth is not meant to cause anxiety or depression but rather to crystallize a plan borne from an understanding of what's at hand. It's designed to help initiate a purpose for your life. That's what this chapter, and for that matter this book, is about. Please don't misunderstand. This isn't about doing a bunch of "stuff" before you die so you won't be left feeling empty. It's about finding joy and the meaning of life by finding *your* purpose.

Let's say you knew when you were going to die. Would the reality of your pending death also come with relief, knowing you had lived a full life and made the absolute best use of your God-given talents? Would you be content in the fact that you had loved your loved ones to the best of your ability? That you had chased as many dreams as you possibly could? Would you be able to look at yourself in the mirror and smile because, although you had just learned the game was in the fourth quarter, you were up by 14 points and had left nothing on the field?

EVERY DAY IS AN EXTRA INNING

I watched the World Series for the first time in probably 20 years in 2017 when the Astros played the Dodgers. I think anyone who watched the series will agree I picked a good series to return to the game of baseball. The entire series was exhausting to watch. It could not have been scripted better by Hollywood. There were no gimmes based on who was at bat or who was pitching. It seemed that anyone at any moment might hit a grand slam. A "sure hitter" could go down watching a strike fly right down the middle of the plate. It was a truly remarkable World Series.

The most intense had to be game 5. The two teams came in with the series at 3 games to 2 in the Astros favor. This game became a slugfest. It seemed every time one team would hit a home run, the other would answer with its own. No fan was safe. Just when you thought your team had pulled off the unspeakable, the other team would answer. It was awesome. Then came the 9th inning. The Dodgers entered the inning down but could rally to not only tie the game but also take the lead. This sent the Astros to the plate with one last chance to tie or win the game. It was an almost sudden-death situation.

The Astros delivered and tied the game, sending the game into extra innings! At this point the entire atmosphere changed. Everything was do or die. If the Dodgers got the lead, they had to maintain it to secure a chance to see another day. If they didn't get a run, every swing of the Astro's bat was a potential loss. The Astros finally won and became the World Champions for the first time in franchise history. As a fifth-generation Texan, I have to say it was pretty darn sweet.

Every day truly is an extra inning. You and I have no idea what inning we're in. We were never guaranteed a full 9, so we must always play as though upon waking every morning we've been given another chance to step up to the plate. Every single day should be viewed as a gift, especially if we're healthy and vibrant.

Abby's diagnosis caused me to be ever-grateful for my own health. I have my sight. My father does not. I have a pancreas that regulates my blood sugar. My daughter does not. I have the air in my lungs. My cousin Clay who was taken from this world at the age of 22, does not. With all I have, why would I not make the most of it? I have to. You have to.

I suggest reading this chapter every time you feel sorry for yourself or feel self-pity creeping in. Remember the game can be called at any time. At least in the game of baseball, we know what inning it is. I dare say if they took the innings out and changed the rules so that the umpire at any time could end the game, baseball would be played much differently. There would still be strategy, but I think the coaches and players would take more chances.

Psalm 103:15-17 says, "As for man, his days are like grass; he flourishes like a flower of the field; for the wind passes over it, and it is gone, and its place knows it no more." You may remember this day, but you will never have it back. Please don't waste it.

I would never suggest living with a fatalistic attitude, but we need a greater sense of urgency. It's worthwhile to wake up and remind yourself, "Yes! I have another at bat. Regardless of what I was afraid of happening yesterday, I made it. Regardless of what I didn't get done yesterday, I have another shot. Regardless of what I didn't try yesterday, today could be the day. I have another at-bat!" Swing!

DO WHAT YOU LOVE

What will you do with your extra innings? We often convince ourselves we need some impressive industry background or some lofty title to prove our self-worth. How is that valuable if you hate what you're doing? One of my favorite do-what-you-love stories involves one of America's favorite beverages: beer. (And you don't have to be a beer drinker to appreciate this story!) Samuel Adams has become almost as well-known as Budweiser or Coors. It wins just about every national and international beer award a beer can win, year after year.

Jim Koch is the founder and CEO of The Boston Brewing Company that produces Samuel Adams beer. He was a Harvard grad and initially pursued a management consultant job for Boston Consulting Group. One day, however, Jim figured out what he was really passionate about and decided to make a living doing it. His family had been brewing beer for years. Using his family recipe, he made a batch of what is now known as Sam Adams Boston Lager. He carried it from pub to pub, trying to get orders. Before long, the very pubs Jim had once cold-called were now calling him for his Boston Lager.

There probably aren't many Harvard grads making beer out there, but Jim is making beer and getting paid for it! Boston Consulting is a top-tier firm with high-paying salaries, so my suspicion is that Jim was making good money even before he ever brewed a batch of Boston Lager for commercial consumption. He realized there was something more profitable than money: doing what you love. I love watching the Sam Adams commercials and seeing the real-life employees enjoy what they are doing for a living.

Take money and the expectations of society out of the equation. Decide what it is that would allow you to put your God-given talents, gifts, and abilities on display and do it! Every dream has its price, but you can't afford to stay where you are.

BURN YOUR SHIPS

Have you ever wondered where the statement, "Burn your ships" comes from? As the story goes, during the conquests of 1519, there was a Spanish explorer named Hernan Cortes. Upon reaching the shores of Vera Cruz, he ordered his men to burn the ships they arrived on. In other words, there would be no turning back. Success wasn't just an option but the only option. I haven't found a way to make something great happen by only being half in. When I decided to launch a life of entrepreneurship, I went all in. I rolled the dice and had no option but to succeed. It's a scary proposition, but it's the only way I know to find out what you are made of. It clears the mind. It forces you to move ahead in spite of circumstances. Therefore, if you are serious about this, burn your ships.

TIME TO GET REAL

1. What do you need to "cut away" in order to grow a fuller and richer life? Be specific.
2. When was a time an uncertain change turned out to be a good thing? What did you learn from that situation?
3. What would it look like for you to "burn the ships"? Where will you light the match?

CHAPTER 7

THE PRICE OF A DREAM

"The mass of men lead lives of quiet desperation."
—HENRY DAVID THOREAU

In the Bible, there is a story of a man walking through a field who finds hidden treasure. He's ecstatic about his discovery, but he knows he can't take it home with him—after all, it's not his property. Therefore, he rushes back and sells everything he has so that he can purchase the land that held the treasure. I have held the treasure of being an owner, not an employee, in my hand. And when I did, I sold out completely and bought that field. Are you willing to risk any price—even the death of your dream—in order to see whether or not you can achieve it? It's an important question, but it has to be asked. You see, most people won't pursue their dreams—and not just because they fear failure. There's something worse. If it doesn't work out as they intended, then something bigger than failure exists. The dream will have died. As long as they never try, they never risk that possibility. People don't want to pay the price of a dead dream, so they're happier just looking at them on paper and doing nothing.

I also carried around a dream to strike out on my own long before I acted on it. At the same time, I experienced the anxiety of wondering if I'd be stepping out, only to fail miserably. If that happened, I would be much less likely to give it a second chance. They say, "If at first you don't succeed try, try again." I like that philosophy, but in reality I'm not wired that way. I think if I had set out on my own and failed, I would be too hesitant to try again.

It's like the story of Abraham and Isaac in the Bible. God asked something of Abraham that many of us would surely have failed to do. One day, the Lord spoke to Abraham and asked him to sacrifice his son, Isaac, on an altar used for animal sacrifices. One can only imagine what this must have been like for Abraham. However, the ever-faithful servant of God did as he was told. Even as he and Isaac began walking to the place where the sacrifice was to take place, Isaac innocently asked his father why they were not carrying a lamb or goat with them, as they had done many times before. Abraham resolutely replied, "The Lord will provide the sacrifice." When they arrived, he took his son in his arms and laid Isaac on the altar. Just as he pulled out his knife, an angel of the Lord spoke up to stop Abraham from killing his own child. Abraham then saw a ram with his horns caught in a thicket and used the ram as the sacrifice instead.

In this instance, God was testing Abraham's faith. I can't even imagine such a challenge. However, God rewarded Abraham's faith. Many of you are coddling your dream as though it's an only child. If you exert any action on the dream, you risk sacrificing it on the altar of failure. But if you fail to follow through on your plans, the dream was nothing sacred to begin with. Don't cling to your dream as though it's something you might be asked to sacrifice. Move forward in faith. What if God wants your dream to "live"?

I didn't want to look back one day wondering what could have been. That thought drove me crazy. Emotionally, I was able to place myself 20 years down the road, and I could sense in my stomach the nauseating feeling I would have then if I had never tried.

One of my favorite pastors, John Piper, wrote a book called *Don't Waste Your Life*. I encourage you to pick it up—it's much better and more meaningful than the book you have in your hands right now! Trust me on this one. Piper mentions a story about a successful couple who had worked hard for years and years. When they were finally able to retire, they purchased a boat and sailed around the world collecting seashells. Sounds good, right? Piper calls it a wasted life. At the end of your days, all you would have is a bunch of seashells to show for it. Don't you want more? I know I do. This is the only life we have, so why waste it? I would rather lose all I've worked for to this point and have the memories of the struggles, the ups, the downs, the good times, and the bad than a bucketful of shells at the end of my life.

I once read a story of an actor who wanted desperately to make it in Hollywood. He was a first-generation immigrant with no money, no connections, and no formal education. But he had a great idea for a movie. In his effort to become an actor and go all in, he ended up broke. However, undaunted he kept pursuing his dream. He had a vision for a movie that he believed with all his heart would be a success.

So broke and desperate, yet so convicted of his dream and vision, he sold his dog to have enough money to continue his pursuit. Eventually, his script was purchased by a studio, and after much haggling, he landed the leading role. This is the story of the lengths Sylvester Stallone went through to realize his dream of making the movie *Rocky*.

This isn't going to be easy. Nothing worthwhile ever is. It will not be comfortable. It will at times be scary as all get out. You may even be made to look a fool. However, settling for "good enough," "being comfortable," and "mediocrity" rarely yields the fruit that the pursuit of a real dream or vision can produce. I can't stress enough that there is a mental, sometimes physical, and almost definitely emotional cost to pursuing your life's ambitions.

TIME IS TICKING

Imagine someone said to you, "For the rest of your life, I'm going to deposit $24,000 a day into a bank account for you. The only stipulation is you must spend it all that day because you can't save it up from one day to the next. The next day, I will fill it with $24,000 more. Again, you must spend it all because I won't let you carry over the balance."

We would never let a penny stay in the account, right? We would find something, anything, to spend the money on. That's how we should treasure our time on earth. Every day we receive 24 hours in our bank account to use however we please. The only catch is we will never get that day's worth back, and we can't carry over into the next day. While there are certain things you must spend the time on, you can take what's left to do exactly what you please and make the absolute most of it. I suggest you keep a journal of your time. How much time do you sleep per night? Watch television? Play on the computer? Count it up—do you need all that time? You are the greatest asset you have. What are you doing to get the most return on that asset?

I'm not saying we need to pack our lives with senseless activities just to fill the void between major events, but we must realize we only have so much time. I want to look back and know I did the most with the time I had. I want to squeeze out every last drop of my potential and use it to the fullest. I want to do as much good for others and my country as I possibly can. I want to give my wife and daughters all the love, time, and attention I possibly can. I don't want to take any of it for granted.

I admit I take this to extremes sometimes. I once ran for City Council, started graduate school at Southern Methodist University in Dallas, ran my company, participated in Leadership Tyler executive training, hosted a weekly radio show and served on several committees, including the Executive Board of the Texas Association of Realtor—all at once. Did I have to do all this? No, but why not do it? If I'm able, and my family doesn't suffer in the process, why shouldn't I?

Right now, it's a hot, lazy August Sunday afternoon. I could turn on the television (the "The Brain Rotter" as we call it in the Wright house), or I could write this book to you. It may be years before you read what I'm writing you now, but I feel it's much more productive than soaking in the abyss of American television.

You would be surprised how much time you have that you aren't using.

Time is like a lot of the useful junk around the house we never use. For instance, most Americans have a Bible somewhere in their homes, whether they're Christians or not. The instruction manual for life is right there in your house somewhere, but when was the last time you picked it up? You have a phone, right? I'm sure you've used it, but when was the last time you used it to call someone you haven't spoken to in years? Someone you know for a fact would be encouraged by hearing from you?

I know something else you have to have in your home. I don't know how we ever survived without this universal appliance before. You have a computer and Internet access, don't you? Did you know you can get a college degree right there from the comfort of your own chair? Did you know you can most likely double your vocabulary with that one little appliance?

Most people won't use their time this way. Most people won't put much of what I'm saying into action. It's a fact. I don't even have to look up statistics to prove it. I just know it. Oh sure, they may get fired up temporarily and make a few changes. Maybe they'll put some goals on paper and write out a little plan, but most won't do so. Will you? Do you value how your friend will feel if you pick up the phone and call? Do you value earning the large vocabulary? Do you value a closer relationship with the Lord of the universe, the Lord of Lords and the King of Kings?

The ones who are willing to do the things most people won't do are the ones working toward a better life. Will you risk the death of your dream in the pursuit of it? Can you handle your stomach turning with anxiety as you figure out how you're going to make this all work? If so, read on.

DO THE THINGS OTHERS AREN'T WILLING TO DO

You must be willing to do the things others won't do. This is one of the single most significant pieces of advice I can give anyone wanting to pursue their dream, passion, or idea. One of the most erroneous things people say is, "I don't have time." What they should say is, "What you are proposing is not important enough to me to make time for." That would be more accurate. For instance, I'm told all the time by out-of-shape people how much they would "love" to exercise, but they just don't have time. That's such a bunch of bull butter. We all have the same amount of time. Some choose not to use it to exercise.

I get up early to work out. At one point, I was getting up before five every morning during the business week to work out. As a result, I lost weight and got into the best shape of my life. Did I like doing that? No, I didn't. Was it hard? It most certainly was. Am I in good shape? You bet I am. I finally determined that being fit and thin meant more to me than two extra hours of sleep. Most people would choose the sleep. It's the easiest and most satisfying. Most people won't get up and work out that hard. That's why most people aren't in top shape. In this area, I'm proving to myself that I'm willing to do the things most people won't do in order to reach my goals.

The opposite of this mindset is the reason most small businesses fail. They are started by people who won't do the things others won't do. They won't fire bad employees. They won't sacrifice a vacation. They won't write their goals on paper. They won't spend time with their employees. They won't spend money to train themselves and their employees. They won't operate without debt. They didn't take the necessary steps to be successful before they even got started. As I heard Andy Stanley once quote, "Discipline, not desire, determines a man's destiny."

In high school, my step-brother always claimed that I didn't have to work as hard as others to be a good football player. He contended I was just a natural athlete. On the other hand, he most definitely was not. He had never been successful in sports. He was right about the fact that God gave me speed and strength, but there's more to it. In the heat of summer, I used to strap tires to my back and drag them across the yard. I would lift weights like a madman. I would swim laps. I ran for miles in the heat of the day. I hated every minute of this. However, I knew most of my opponents weren't doing these things and I would have the upper hand. On the flip side, my better opponents were most definitely doing these things, and I sure didn't want them to have the upper hand. Could my step-brother have been a good athlete? I don't know. However, I know for a fact he never strapped a tire to his back and carried it anywhere! As a result, I was an All-State football player, and he most certainly was not.

We love stories of people who seem to have an extra dose of grit and determination that almost makes them seem superhuman. One such individual I've recently discovered is David Goggins. Goggins is a retired Navy SEAL and is the only member of the U.S. Armed Forces to complete SEAL training (including two Hell Weeks), the U.S. Army Ranger School (where he graduated as Enlisted Honor Man) and Air Force Tactical Air Controller training. Goggins is also one of the most prolific ultra-endurance athletes in the world. According to his official website (www.davidgoggins.com) Goggins has completed over 60 ultra-marathons, triathlons, and ultra-triathlons, setting new course records and regularly placing in the top five. He once held the Guinness World Record for pull-ups, completing 4,030 in 17 hours. However, Goggins grew up poor, shy, and overweight. It wasn't until he was almost 300 pounds and in horrible shape that he decided to turn his life around.

One of my favorite quotes from Goggins is, "We all want to take this four-lane highway, but we always step over the shovel. All I did was pick up that shovel and dig my own path." That is the essence of success. Pick up the shovel and dig your path. Shoveling isn't easy. In fact, shoveling can be downright awful. However, it's often the only way to create the path we so desperately need to realize our mission.

This truth reminds me of an ancient story I once read that teaches the value of doing what you feel you must do, regardless of what others do or don't do.

The Boulder in the Road

Once upon a time there was a king who controlled a large kingdom. One night when it was very dark, he had a large boulder placed in the center of one of the major roadways. The king awoke early the next morning and hid in the trees alongside the road. He wanted to watch what people would do when they came upon the large rock blocking their path.

The first to come down the road were the wealthy merchants and courtiers of the king's court who were going to work. When they saw the large rock blocking their path, they all stopped to complain loudly but did nothing to move the rock.

They blamed the king for not taking care of the roads for which they all paid taxes to have maintained. They felt the king was negligent in not keeping the roads clear. When they were done complaining, they walked around the boulder and went on their way.

An hour passed and along came a peasant carrying a large basket of vegetables he was taking to the market to sell. When he approached the boulder, he laid down his basket and tried desperately to move the large rock out of the way. Unable to move the stone, he walked into the woods and found a large piece of wood which he could use as a lever. After much straining, he and his lever succeeded in rolling the boulder out of the way and to the side of the road.

When he turned to pick up his basket of vegetables, he noticed a beautiful silk purse lying in the center of the road where the boulder had been. Upon opening the purse, he saw 50 gold coins and a handwritten note signed by the king. The king's note indicated the 50 gold coins were a reward for the person or persons who removed the boulder from the roadway.

It was the King's hope to teach his subjects a valuable lesson. Those who do something good for the community where they live, such as removing obstacles or improving the conditions for others, are always rewarded for their efforts in the end.

There is a reward for those who will do the things others won't. Most people won't strike out on their own. Most people won't lose the 30 pounds they need to lose. Most people won't stop drinking. Most people won't give up whatever vice they have that could be ruining their life or family. Most people will do what is comfortable. Most people will stay on the four-lane road instead of picking up the shovel. That's what sets us apart. We WILL do what others won't. While they are complaining about the universe being against them, we will dig and dig until our path is realized.

It often doesn't take a lot of brains or guts to succeed. It just takes a willingness to try. Consider the success of people who were willing to do what others wouldn't. Waste Management, the world's largest trash collector, saw a job no one else wanted to do and wrote a business plan to do it. They make millions every week. MLB star Don Mattingly would take 500 cuts off a tee before every baseball game. Dennis Rodman had a three-hour post-game workout in the NBA. Olympian Michael Phelps swam laps every day, even on Christmas and Thanksgiving. These people did the things others won't. As a result, they achieved immense success.

Does hard work and sacrifice guarantee success? It most certainly does not. If there were a proven formula for 100% success, it wouldn't be rare or scarce, this success we are talking about. However, like Teddy Roosevelt said, "It is not the critic who counts; not the man who points out how the strong man stumbles, or where the doer of deeds could have done them better. The credit belongs to the man who is actually in the arena, whose face is marred by dust and sweat and blood; who strives valiantly; who errs, who comes short again and again, because there is no effort without error and shortcoming; but who does actually strive to do the deeds; who knows great enthusiasms, the great devotions; who spends himself in a worthy cause; who at the best knows in the end the triumph of high achievement, and who at the worst, if he fails, at least fails while daring greatly, so that his place shall never be with those cold and timid souls who neither know victory nor defeat."

TIME TO GET REAL

1. Write down all the ways uncertainty is keeping you from stepping out in faith. Study your list and scratch through each item until you

can no longer read it. What if all your uncertainty went away, just like that?

2. If there is some huge obstacle keeping you from pursuing your dream, sit down and write out how you could make the obstacle part of the path. This requires extreme focus. I didn't have the money to purchase my first company. That was a huge obstacle. Therefore, borrowing the seller's equity in his building became the way.

3. You can do anything for a week, so journal your daily activity for the next 7 days. Find the "white space" you can devote to pursuing your ambitions. What did you learn about yourself and your goals at the end of 7 days?

CHAPTER 8

YOU, INC.

"It is not length of life, but depth of life."
—RALPH WALDO EMERSON

Would you believe my editor and I almost used the title of this chapter as the title of the book? I must admit I liked it at first. Despite sounding somewhat self-serving, it makes sense. Many of us take ourselves for granted. When we consider our business plans and life goals, we forget to prepare ourselves for whatever it is we wish to endeavor.

Let's think about how you treat your car for a second. Would you ever drive your car for 5,000 miles without stopping? Fill the gas tank with dirt and the engine with toothpaste instead of oil? Never wash it, rotate the tires, or only replace the fluids after they ran completely out? Of course not. Let's contrast that with how many people treat their bodies. Instead of water, we pour soda, coffee, or whatever else down our throats. Instead of nutritious food for fuel, we turn to greasy, fat-filled, quick-and-easy stuff. We neglect our outward appearance by not giving ourselves the nutrients we need for healthy skin. We wear our muscles down with the daily rigors of life and never move them around to keep them fresh. We don't take a sip of water until we are thirsty, thus having reached the first level of dehydration.

However, we will spend thousands of dollars on a new laptop or software. We will make sure we have the latest and greatest PDA or cell phone. We justify these things as business necessities, because they are the tools that help us get the job done. Well, think about this, Buster Brown. Which machine are you using to control the machines? You! Which machine houses your personal CPU? Your body does. Which machine controls whether you make that one extra cold call or knock out that one extra listing presentation? That's right, Sparky, it's your body! Don't you think you might want to spend just a little time taking care of that machine? To me, it's just common sense. Why would you care so little about something of such magnificent importance?

YOUR GREATEST INVESTMENT

You simply cannot neglect investing in "you"—intellectually, physically, and spiritually. Focus on sharpening these three things that make up who you are, and you will sharply increase your chances of success.

Get intellectually fit

Our intellectual investment is one of the most neglected areas. I think so many are doing the bare minimums in life. For instance, we learned algebra just because we had to, in order to get through school. Now we read manuals because we need to know how to do something at work. Why don't we learn just because we can?

One of my biggest pet peeves is how little people know about American history. We are living in the greatest country on planet earth, and so few people even know what's so great about it. That's a shame because we look at things the wrong way. We only know what we "have to know" to survive. Why not strive to know more, considering humans have a greater ability to learn than any other species of animal on earth? Why not learn another language just because you can? Why not take a course or two online in a subject that interests you?

Read, read, read. Smart and successful people read. Once when asked what his favorite piece of technology was, marketing guru and best-selling author Seth Godin replied, "books." He is so right. In many cases for less than a Starbucks drink, you can own the life work of a genius. You can be taken to a foreign land. You can learn about an industry. It's amazing. It's also the best exercise for your brain. The brain is like any other muscle. It needs to be flexed to stay strong. Therefore, I can't tell you enough, read! I will include in the appendix a list of my favorite and most influential books.

What does any of this have to do with pushing play on your life? How does it affect pursuing a life you never thought possible? It makes you start realizing life was meant to be lived. It makes you realize you can climb into the driver's seat and act, instead of react. It makes life a game. What if, in the grand scheme of things, God really wanted us to enjoy this life? Sound crazy? I don't think so either. Turn the whole system on its head by deciding you want to live, not just wait around to die.

I love to say I'm semi-retired. This just blows people away because I'm relatively young. However, to say I have a job is an overstatement. I have a life that includes work. I've created ways to live life instead of just react to it. For example, it's 3:00 p.m. on a Wednesday afternoon, and I'm writing a book at my desk. If I had a "job," I couldn't do that, could I? I made some bold choices, and now I have a life. Do I have responsibilities in my work that I have to do? Well, of course, I do. However, I'm not using this time to write you a book because I have to. I'm using it to write you a book because I can! What could you be doing right now that you aren't just because you have determined you don't "have to" and therefore you never do it?

I'm a firm believer in self-education. I love the movie *Good Will Hunting* about a self-taught genius and recluse who works as a janitor at MIT. Will Hunting has a gift for math and love learning for learning's sake, not because it's required for his lucrative corporate job. It made me want to go out and start doing some high-level calculus or something! Not because I had to, but to the contrary because I don't have to. I could learn it just because I want to! We use so much of our extra time just rotting—soaking up television, reading mind-numbing novels, or flipping through meaningless magazines.

Why not do something we could feel good about afterward?

I went back to school later in life and received an MBA from Southern Methodist University. Did I have to have a secondary degree? Nope, I sure didn't. I did it because I wanted to do it. I'm going to continue to invest in myself the rest of my life and get the most out of "me" before it's too late. I'm going to keep learning because I can, not because I have to.

Get physically fit

Yep, I'm about to throw dirt all in your Cheerios if you are a couch potato. Do me a favor. Take a look around the next time you're out and about. Check out the physical make up of most of the people you see. Most people are carrying around varying degrees of excess weight—some to the extreme.

Americans have become the poster country for indulging in high-fat, high-calorie foods. What you don't necessarily see outwardly is that many overweight people are most likely depressed, have high blood pressure, and suffer fatigue. Here we are a nation where the personal fitness industry flourishes, yet we have a nation full of couch potatoes? What is up? I'll tell you what is up. We are letting our life run us instead of running our lives. Also, we don't look at physical fitness the right way.

I'm a fit guy. I take care of myself. Many say things to me like, "Man, you been hitting the gym?"—as though I'm doing something so out of the ordinary! Granted, I'm a little different than the average bear. I'm an Adonis, so it's no wonder I get comments. I'm just kidding. Take back that "Oh Lord," you just muttered under your breath.

The fact is, exercising and or weight training is the closest thing I have to a hobby. I love to exercise, and there are many reasons why—the least of which is vanity. I like to feel good. I like to wear the clothes I like. I hate lard on my body. I like to have energy. Now I have a Peloton. This has really taken things up a notch. I don't play golf. I don't hunt, fish, or have a standing poker game. However, try to interrupt my scheduled Peloton ride, and I'm fussy. That's right, fussy. I get downright fussy. (I just love writing "fussy." Say it. It's a great word," fussy." Okay, enough.)

I also like the clarity of mind that comes with good health. I like to be attractive to my wife (though I know she would consider me attractive, no matter how I look. At least that's what she tells me. Oh, and she did give me the Peloton. Coincidence? Hmm.) Finally, yes, there is the vanity aspect. I want to look good, and I don't think there is one thing wrong with that—as long as I don't let it become an obsessive pursuit, causing me to neglect more important priorities.

Another huge aspect of physical fitness is that I love the discipline it requires. I love the fact that I have to manage myself. I like keeping track of the calories, carbs, and grams of fat that hit my mouth, because it proves to me that I can manage myself. And it shows others. I know we don't like to be judged, but people are human. They are going to size you up the minute they see you. Let me disclose that I am not a dietician. I'm not a personal trainer, nor have I ever been. However, I do have a brain, and I can read. Every health expert, both MD and non-professional alike, agrees that exercise raises your endorphin levels. This is the hormone that makes you feel happy. Therefore, exercise is a great way to fight depression. Do you think it's any coincidence that America is not only the most obese country on earth, but it's also the most depressed? There are a lot of reasons for our depression that have nothing to do with us cornering the market on couch potatoes, but I would be willing to bet it is a strong contributor.

Some of you are forming the arguments in your head. You're already getting defensive, and I haven't even stated my case completely. So just chill out, and read on. Many of you already realize the benefits of physical fitness, so you should use this as confirmation. Hopefully, you will be reassured in your efforts and keep it up.

Being active has always been part of my DNA, but I didn't always place such high importance on exercise. When I started working, I did just like so many do—I fell into the idea that working out was for people who were on diets, going through a mid-life crisis, or just plain weird. I never placed the level of importance on it that I should have. I certainly never looked at taking time to go the gym as part of being a successful businessperson.

That's because, like many of you, I looked at going to the gym as a luxury, not a necessity. That's where we mess up. Many of us think of gym rats as either super vain people or just the lucky ones that get to go work out. Regardless of their reason for being there, they are probably happier, have more energy, and possibly even look better than most of those who don't exercise. We have to shake free from the idea that physical fitness is only something you do to look good. It's not just a luxury. It's an absolute necessity.

We have been taught that fitness is a vain, selfish indulgence. That's not true at all. Here's what I used to do. Years ago, I had an almost phobic view of leaving the office to go to the gym during the middle of the day. I thought the building would burn down if my ever-so-important presence was void for a couple of hours. I would get to the gym, get a call on my cell, and leave. I just couldn't stay at the gym. Finally, I realized how stupid this behavior was. Not only was I not nearly as needed as I like to think I am at the office, but I was also in need of my workouts. Therefore, I began to divorce myself from my business for at least an hour-and-a-half every day to take care of the machine, my greatest money-making venture and my most prized business tool—me. This has had a huge payoff. I always came back energized. My head was clear. I was more relaxed. My day was broken up nicely, and I felt better.

Many of you reading this simply can't leave your office for the gym. I understand, and to be honest, I don't do it anymore either because I no longer drive to an office. Instead, I'm up at four each morning and working out by five. I exercise for a minimum of one hour a day, six days a week. I've run into people who say, "Boy, it must be nice to work out and stay in shape. I just don't have the time." To that I ask, "What are you so busy doing at 5:00 a.m.?"

They're sleeping.

I didn't say this was easy. If someone says, "I don't have time to exercise," I reply, "Yes you do, but you are choosing to do something else with that time." Stephen Covey brought this to my attention in *The Seven Habits of Highly Effective People* where he notes that we need to own the things we do and don't do. Your physical fitness is every bit as important as your education, your sales training, or whatever it is you are investing in to better yourself. Make physical fitness a part of your business plan.

If you don't want to join a gym, I have a solution for you since I've become much more of a home fitness kind of guy. I do the Tony Horton P90X workout. This is an amazing program. However, it's really intense, so you might want to try one of Tony's other programs. Just go to www.beachbody.com. Their programs are, in my opinion, the highest quality on the market, and Tony is a rock star. Let me also add that I don't work for Beach Body. I don't know anyone at Beach Body, and I get nothing for recommending them. I merely think it's a great company. Shaun T is another of their trainers I enjoy. The aforementioned Peloton has an app in addition to the bike with streamed classes for Yoga, meditation, cardio, boot camp, running, and stretching. You can literally keep your trainer in your pocket at all times. I've worked out in parking garages, hotel rooms, my living room, balconies, you name it. There is just no excuse not to do something physical every day, so please, even if it's just a 20-minute walk get out there.

Physical training also makes you live longer. Let's say you are the average or "normal" weight for your frame and age. According to a study done by lifescience.com, "Normal-weight people who exercised for 150 minutes or more weekly lived about 4.7 years longer than normal-weight people who did not do regular, moderate exercise." I don't think this is a point to belabor. You know you need physical exercise. We all do. If I could compel you to do just one thing it would be to take a walk. Just start by taking a daily 20-minute walk. Don't take your phone. Don't even listen to a book. Just walk and clear your head. The key is to get yourself moving.

Winston Churchill, one of my heroes, would take a bath in the middle of the day every day. This routine kept him fresh during both halves of the day, and if you know anything about Sir Winston, then you know he could churn out some work. John D. Rockefeller took naps regularly. It's okay to take care of yourself. Eat right; get plenty of sleep and exercise. It's a huge part of your success.

Get spiritually fit

I'm going to try to keep this as broad as possible. I've been pretty overt in the fact I'm a born-again Christian, so it goes without saying my spiritual growth is related to a Christian point of view. However, there are other ways to feed your spiritual side. For those of you who are atheist, deist or just-not-sure-ist, why don't you spend some time meditating? I've got an idea, just sit quietly and pray as though God were real. You might be surprised. It's imperative that you feed your spirit regardless of how you do it. Carve out some time where you do absolutely nothing but think all those deep thoughts about life. Try to put some reason and action behind them.

Naturally, it's my heart's desire that you spend time with God and learn who he is, because if you understand God, then you can understand "you" in a way you never have before. After all, I believe he made you and me, so if we can tap into what he's all about, we can then start to understand ourselves better.

How do you know God? Read. I can't tell you how important this is. Read about the things of God and what he's done. Even the non-believer can benefit from the teachings of the Bible. I think it's tragic that many people say they don't believe in God. Or they are just lukewarm Christians who have never even explored what all the fuss is about. Why has no other man on earth ever touched so many lives as Jesus Christ? Go find out. However you want to do it, spend time every day in prayer and meditation. This life is a lot bigger than you and me. Take time to feed your curiosity and nourish your spiritual side.

JUST IN CASE

Just in case some are confused after this chapter (since, on the surface, it doesn't overtly deal with conquering your dream or becoming an entrepreneur) let me clear it up. All I'm saying is that your life shouldn't be about your vocation. Your life should be about...your life! So many of us think our job or vocation is what defines us. Somewhere along the way, we let that happen. A guy with a high school education can be a scholar if he knows enough about a given matter. Why? Because he made it his life's work to do so—not because a piece of paper told him he was.

This is all about chasing and grabbing a life beyond a job, folks. Maybe in the pursuit of this life, you do change jobs. Maybe you don't. Maybe nothing changes except your perspective on the matter. It's not about finding the perfect job. It's about finding a content life that no job can take away from you.

TIME TO GET REAL

Reflect on what's different about you at the end of the month after the following exercises. What's changed? What was difficult? What's getting easier?

1. Keep a food journal for a week and take inventory of just how good/bad your eating habits are. Be
2. If you aren't doing anything physical, go for a walk at least three times a week for a month. If you already have a physical training plan, focus your efforts more on it for one month.
3. Read one book over the next month.
4. Meditate or, at a minimum, make a point to sit still in total silence for five minutes for at least three days per week for a month.

CHAPTER 9

WHAT WE REALLY WANT

"Life is half spent before we know what it is."
—GEORGE HERBERT

From ancient times to the present, these two forces have been colliding: joy and happiness. We've talked about them a lot so far in this book because so many people confuse the two by putting them in the same category. But they are so very far apart. I don't put a lot of stock in "happy." Happy is a temporary emotion that many in today's society seem to be addicted to. "Happy" is, by nature, temporary. Even so, we constantly attempt to make what is undeniably temporary permanent. Like an addict, we will often become numb to what once made us happy and thus continually raise the bar of what it takes to feel happy until nothing works anymore. Many try drugs or other things to remove themselves, if only for a moment, from this world. Some people give up on being happy after many failed attempts and settle into depression. Happiness without joy can only lead to a downfall of one kind or another.

People say you can't buy happiness. That's a crock. You most certainly can. You can buy almost anything, and happy is definitely out there for purchase. If you're utterly miserable with yourself and you have enough money, you can buy a drug, a new car, new clothes, or any number of products or experiences and be happy. For a moment. The only problem is, whatever it took to make you happy is fleeting. In one minute, it will be gone, leaving you right back where you were.

Happiness is often mistaken for joy, and I like to think of it as fool's gold—a worthless yellow mineral that appears to be real gold. Like most things of great value, joy is much harder to come by. It's a little harder to recognize. And, unlike happiness, it can't be purchased, traded or given. It has no price tag. Granted, it comes in varying quantities, but once you have it and recognize it, you can nurture it to secure it for good.

Happiness results from an external matter. It's some material item. It's a drug we put in our bodies. Joy, however, starts from within. This is what protects it from the fickleness of circumstances. It resides deep inside you where nothing can get to it—unless you let it inside. What will amaze you is how simple joy is. And, by the way, happiness is a manifestation of joy—that's thrown in from time to time. Just don't settle for something as minute and temporary as happiness alone. Understand what it takes to go for the good stuff that lasts and get yourself a big dose of joy.

VISITING THE WORLD'S BIGGEST TOY STORE

Do you remember when you were a kid begging your parents to take you to the toy store so you could marvel at all the delightful things on the shelves? Everything was there for the taking—shiny little cars, beautiful dolls, and an assortment of gadgets and gizmos all promising hours and hours of entertainment. Of course, whenever we brought one of these treasures home, the newness and excitement quickly wore off and we were soon back to begging our parents for another trip to Toys R Us.

When we grow up, we don't stop going to the toy store. To the contrary, the store just gets bigger and we don't need Mom and Dad to take us anymore. Adults live in the world's biggest toy store, and the streets on which we drive are the aisles. We think if we can just get enough of this stuff—a bigger this, a faster that—we will be happy.

All day long, we are being sold happiness. A pill will make us men better lovers, we're told. A new car will make us more exciting. According to the commercials, if I drink a diet drink on roller skates, I might find myself living in the middle of a music video! I often wonder what it would be like if I suddenly broke out and started living my very own personal Broadway musical like I see people do on television commercials. You know, what if I just sang all my answers to people who ask me questions? When the phone rings, I imagine myself singing out, "I gotta get it! I just gotta get it! Everyone now watch me get this phooooone." Wouldn't that be great? Okay, I'll get back in great writer mode.

The point is that adults spend their time in the world's biggest toy store, feeding their addiction to happy. They buy big houses, fast motorcycles, and fancy cars. And when those things are no longer big, fast, or fancy enough—they buy the next size up. I have no problem with anyone having nice things. That's none of my business. I just thank God I don't require those things to feel fulfilled. Have you ever wondered why some of the richest, most powerful people in the world are so miserable? It's because they've been duped. They thought they could buy lasting joy, and instead just ended up with a bunch of happy. Don't fall for that bait-and-switch scheme.

There's not much of anything you can buy and put in your life, literally or figuratively, that is going to result in lasting happiness or joy. Sorry, tiger. You're going to have to work for it. You will be amazed when you lead a life of joy how fruitless the pursuit of happy really was. Don't waste your life addicted to happy. There is something better.

TAKE A LOOK INSIDE

When you set out to have an incredible life filled with joy, you become more alien to the toy store mentality. Then, and this is really sweet, it will take a lot less of the stuff in the toy store to make you happy. You might not even need it anymore. If you don't need it, then you might not have to make all that money you thought you did. If you don't have to make all that money, you might finally be able to take the lower-paying job that keeps you home at night. And, all told, you might find the job is something you actually enjoy. Get it? En-joy! Now we're making things happen, people!

Let's check to see what God thinks of joy versus happy. According to my research, "joy" is mentioned in the Bible some 165 times. As for "happy," it is mentioned a paltry 25. A great illustration of joy is in one of my favorite movies, *The Shawshank Redemption*, starring Tim Robbins as a banker named Andy Dufresne who is falsely accused and imprisoned for murdering his wife's lover. After years in prison, Andy petitions Congress to buy books for a prison library so he and the inmates can learn while serving their time. After faithfully writing letters every week, some boxes with books and music records finally show up.

In one of the boxes, Andy finds an opera record. He puts the music on and proceeds to play it over the loudspeakers of the prison. He locks himself inside the office until the meanest guard in the prison breaks in and stops the music. For punishment, Andy is sent to solitary confinement. Upon his release, he enters the cafeteria where his fellow inmates are eating. Immediately, the others want to know how Andy's time in the hole was. Surprisingly, he admits it was the easiest time he'd ever done. The other prisoners are skeptical. He then tells them the beauty of music is that it's inside you, in a place others can't touch. Neither the guards nor anyone else could take it away from Andy. Joy is the same way. Once you have it inside, no one and nothing can touch it.

If you suddenly lost all the external stimulation it takes to make you happy—your house, your car, your job, your bank account, and even your physical body—and all you had left was what was inside of you, what would we find there? If you could no longer buy happiness, would there be any joy inside to sustain you? Can you imagine being alive, but being left with nothing except what's inside your soul?

I read a story about a young teen that was hurt in a bicycle accident and became a quadriplegic. Over the years, as he struggled to complete rehab and reclaim his life, he discovered the only thing he had control over was what was left inside of him. His body was paralyzed, but his soul was alive.

He did not allow his circumstances to take away his joy. He completed high school, went to college, and now pursues life to its fullest from a wheelchair, even scuba-diving with the aid of a second diver.

Happiness can be taken away from you in a moment's notice. But can you lose your joy? Of course, you can! But if you do, you have allowed something to take its place. No one else is to blame. If you find the life you want, you will more than likely discover some measure of joy to go with it.

WHAT WE REALLY WANT

I love telling the story of how I became a real estate broker. When I was five, my mother asked me what I wanted to be when I grew up. I looked up with a sparkle in my eye with fists clenched and almost shouted, "Mommy, I want to be a real estate broker!" Of course, this is hogwash. I never once in my life said I wanted to be a real estate broker. Nor did I ever say I wanted to be an entry-level consultant, or a headhunter, or any of the other jobs I have had through the years. I have to remind you there were days I hated being a real estate broker. This was my day job, but most of the time, I found it about as interesting as selling cotton candy. However, while I may not have been crazy about my vocation at the time, I was crazy about the life I started to lead.

At the genesis of my corporate career I had a great job in the part of Houston I loved. Living in the same neighborhood as my in-laws at that time, as crazy as it sounds, was my utopia. However, I wanted to quit my job. I wasn't alert enough to see I had a job that had given me exactly the life I wanted. As a result, I spent years bouncing from place to place, looking for the perfect job situation, not once considering the right "life" situation. What I wanted was a better life—I just didn't know it. Hopefully, you're beginning to see by now that you don't have to leave your current job. Just put your current job in its proper position in your list of priorities. I honestly think if I had done so in my first year of work after college, I wouldn't have left my first job all those years ago. I was looking for all the wrong things to fulfill me as it related to my career.

As I said earlier, I'm on the backside of complexity in this matter, which is why it seems so simple to me now. I messed it up early on before I knew better. You don't have to follow my example. Start carving out your ideal life now. Many of you might be living the life of your dreams right now, you just don't know it. You're so focused on the job that you aren't looking at the life that comes with it. Certainly, there are cases where the job you've chosen is a big factor in why you can't live the life you want. And it may be necessary for you to leave. However, not everyone needs to leave their job to have a life they love. It wasn't until after my job at The Home Depot that I stopped looking for a great life through a job. Instead, I started looking for a great life and plugging a job into the equation.

Focus on the *life* you want to live. Once you do this, you will be amazed at how little some of the greatest things in life cost. For instance, I mentioned that one of the most satisfying aspects of my new life as a broker was not having to travel so I could be home every night for dinner. That didn't cost a penny. However, under the old mindset, I was just looking for eight hours of happiness during a workday instead of joy in a fulfilled 24 hours. Do you see the difference?

A job is merely what pays for the life. I have a great life and a job that suits my idea of a great life. That's what I want for you. The first step is getting your mind off having some incredible job or career that will make you happy. Only a fulfilled life will bring you joy (which we've established is what you're really looking for). Here's what else I don't mind about this new life I have. Within minutes of writing this line, I received a phone call. I've been trying to land an interview for my *Texas Titans* podcast with Dr. Ruth Simmons. Dr. Simmons is currently the president of Prairie View A&M University and the former of Brown University. She was the first African American to be the president of an Ivy League school. I will have to drive 3.5 hours to do this interview. I won't be paid a penny for it. I will turn around and drive back the very same day. However, it doesn't bother me at all. I'm trying to build my *Texas Titans* podcast into a monetizable venture. Therefore, I will go with glee.

LESSONS FROM AN AUTO MECHANIC AND A FISHERMAN

I think auto mechanics have it figured out. First, they have a universally-needed skill, which not all of us can say. Second, they don't have to deal with people for the most part. They work on their autos until they are fixed and move on. They make a respectable wage. And most of them have weekends off. When the day is over, they leave their work in the garage. Most of them are car nuts, too, so they get to mix vocation with passion. All in all, I think auto mechanics do pretty well. Think for a second how much your respect and cherish a trusted mechanic. These folks are truly special.

I bet if you asked a mechanic if he was living the best life he could imagine, he would probably look at you like you were crazy. However, you have to admit he's got it pretty good. Life's not all that complicated. Being able to enjoy it is not that complicated either. We complicate it by following the methods set forth by a bunch of other people who don't know how to enjoy life either. I'm reminded of one of my favorite fables that could sum up this whole book, but it wouldn't make me look nearly as smart, so I'm writing all this other stuff.

An American businessman was visiting a small coastal Panamanian village. He saw a small boat with just one fisherman docked. Inside the boat were several large yellowfin tuna. The American complimented the fisherman on the quality of his fish and asked how long it took to catch them.

"Only a little while," the fisherman said.

The American then asked why he didn't stay out longer and catch more fish. The fisherman said he had enough to support his family's immediate needs.

"But what do you do with the rest of your time?" the American wanted to know.

"I sleep late, fish a little, play with my children, take siesta with my wife, and stroll into the village each evening where I sip wine and play guitar with my amigos. I have a full and busy life."

The American scoffed, "I am a Wall Street executive and I can help you.

You should spend more time fishing and with the proceeds buy a bigger boat and get a web presence. A scalable go-forward plan would provide capital for several new boats. Eventually, you would have a fleet of fishing boats. Instead of selling your catch to a middleman, you would sell directly to the processor, eventually opening your own cannery. You would control the product, processing, and distribution. Of course, you would need to move to Panama City, then Los Angeles, and eventually New York. There, you would outsource tasks to third party clients to help run your expanding enterprise in a vertical market."

"But how long will this all take?" the fisherman asked.

The American replied, "Only 15 to 20 years."

"But what then?"

The American laughed and said, "That's the best part. When the time is right, you will announce an IPO, sell your company stock to the public, and become very rich. You will make millions."

"Millions, Señor? Then what?"

The American smiled and said proudly, "Well, then you will retire, move to a small coastal fishing village where you can sleep late, fish a little, play with your kids, take siesta with your wife, and stroll to the village in the evenings where you will sip wine and play guitar with your amigos."

WHAT'S MISSING

So much of life is perspective. Take a good, hard look at what you want in life and envision what's missing. It might be right under your nose, and you just haven't realized it yet. So much of our lives could be more fulfilling if we will take the time to evaluate what we want. We will search far and wide for the perfect car. We will go to great lengths to research the perfect vacation spot. We will wring our hands over choosing the right house plans for the home of our dreams. Why not take the time to evaluate what could lead to a lifetime of fulfillment and joy?

I think the best stories are the ones based in reality. In the next chapter, you'll meet real-life people who were forced to get out and start living the best life they possibly could. They all share something in common. They began living life the way they wanted at the worst possible time.

TIME TO GET REAL

1. Define the word "content" as it relates to you. Ask your best friend what he/she thinks contentment looks like to you. Are the two definitions similar or different? What does this reveal about you?
2. Close your eyes and search your life for a time you felt pure joy from an experience, not a "thing." If you suddenly lost all the external stimulation it takes to make you happy, and all you had left was what was inside of you, what would we find there?
3. Can you stay in your current job and design the life you truly want? If yes, how? If not, what are you willing to do about it?

CHAPTER 10

THE BEST CATASTROPHE THAT EVER HAPPENED!

"Success is going from failure to failure without a loss of enthusiasm."
—WINSTON CHURCHILL

There is a reason why the adage "sink or swim" is so popular. At the end of the day, that's what many of us are going to do. We are either going to sink or swim. Many of you reading this may be facing a do-or-die situation right now. You may be unemployed or will soon be out of a job. You may be facing a mountain of debt or going through some crisis in one form or another.

First, I want to encourage you. This crisis may be the greatest thing that ever happened to you. I know, I know. It doesn't make you feel one bit better about the fact that you don't know if you will be able to make the mortgage payment this month. Think of it this way: you have nowhere to go but up. Nothing makes you appreciate having plenty like having nothing. If you are at the bottom right now, look around. Are you still alive? Are you fed? I didn't ask if you were eating the rich food you prefer. I just asked if you were fed. Do you still have a family? If you are able to answer "yes" to these things, then you are in what might be the best place you will ever be. You're down in the valley, and it's in the valley where the good stuff grows. I have been there, and I know it's true.

This is the perfect time for some transparency. One of the greatest catastrophes in my life was my divorce. I'm a man who prided himself on being the perfect husband and father. The thought of my children growing up in a broken home was devastating to me. After my divorce, I vowed I would never marry again. I felt like a recluse. After my failed run for Congress, I was even more embarrassed. I decided I had to make some huge changes and get back to the guy who wrote *Push Play*.

Being a real estate broker is what I knew, so I started there. Another real estate company named WP & Co. I had co-founded was still around, and my wonderful partner, Chris, had only grown the business since I left.

Therefore, I decided I'd renew my broker's license and see if real estate was what I needed to do again. While taking a continuing education class at the Greater Tyler Association of Realtors, I ran into a friend I had not seen in years. She didn't know I was divorced and immediately began playing matchmaker. She told me about a girl who was younger than me, never married, owned her own business, loved the Lord, and happened to be beautiful. Even with such an enticing description, I didn't take the bait and said, "I'm sorry, Pam. I'm just not interested in dating anyone. Rylan and Abby are the only women in my life for the foreseeable future. Thank you just the same."

I thought about my response afterward for a long time. Did I honestly want to live alone? Was it simply a fear of failure keeping me from at least meeting someone else? I decided to go against my instincts. I called Pam up and asked for the girl in question's phone number. Pam called back saying Jemilynn had said she'd think about my request. I later learned this wasn't the case. Pam was sparing my feelings. Jemilynn had actually told Pam, "Thanks, but no thanks." I was okay, though. While I felt rejected, I was at least pleased I had tried.

About two days later, Pam texted me and asked if I'd give her a call about "our little project." Jemilynn had eventually agreed to go to coffee and told Pam she could share her number with me! When I received Pam's text, I was on the beach in Destin where the girls and I have spent the past 10 summers. I was surprisingly excited. I wasn't sure if this would lead to anything and wasn't certain I wanted it to. However, I was looking forward to the new adventure. It's amazing how making a decision and then seeing progress, one way or the other, can bring a bit of satisfaction. I was happy something new might be in the works. It meant I was still alive.

Jemilynn still had no interest in going on a date or dating anyone. However, after a stern talking-to from these friends (to whom I will forever be indebted to), she had agreed to have a 30-minute coffee. As I sat at Strada coffeehouse waiting for Jemilynn, my stomach danced with butterflies. At Jemilynn's standard seven minutes late for everything, she arrived.

"My Lord, she's beautiful," I thought to myself.

I played it cool, but man I was taken by her beauty. Then she spoke. I have no idea why, and to this day she laughs when I tell her, but her voice is the most amazing thing I've ever heard. Our 30-minute coffee turned into an hour and a half. I can't even recall what we discussed. All I know is that I was mesmerized. She was articulate, gorgeous, and I was bowled over.

Not once did I think of all the pain and misery that had led me to singlehood. No negative thought could penetrate my mind in her presence. There was only this sense of being in the presence of the greatest gift God had ever sat before me. I was done that quickly. We saw each other off and on for the next week. Then her nephew came to stay with her to provide a nice buffer and relieve us from any awkward, "so what do we do now moments." One week from the day we had our first coffee, I decided I was going to marry Jemilynn McKee and make her Mrs. Jason Wright. However, I knew I couldn't tell her that. I couldn't tell anyone. They'd think I was crazy. Therefore, I started Jemilynn a journal and professed my love daily until 129 days later, when I asked her to be my wife. Here is my journal entry after one week:

7/20/18

No one writes letters anymore, and I think that's a shame. Everything is handled by text or DM or some other digital means that allows for immediate communication. I think letters are good because they require thought and consideration. As such, I wanted to take the time to write you one. I will try to be brief and to the point because letters by their very nature tend to expand a point beyond what's necessary for conveyance. If I fail to reach this goal, please forgive me.

First, I'm normally given to look at something like this and automatically regret it not happening sooner. For instance, you've been here all along. I've been here all along. Yet we never crossed paths. However, I don't think that way at all. I've become so in tune with the fact that God has us exactly where he wants us, when he wants us there, and I know the timing for our meeting was absolutely ordained by Heaven. I don't doubt it for a second.

I know God has blessed our meeting because I want nothing for myself in this. All I want is to give. I can see God's light in you so very clearly. I see nothing but sweetness, and kindness, and beauty. My greatest desire is to make you smile. I want to make you feel safe, secure, loved, and adored. I said I would most likely never be with anyone again because my standards were so very high. In fact, I think I even set them ridiculously high to protect myself. Then you came along. You hit every heretofore unreachable standard and then some.

I'm going to marry you, Jemilynn. You are going to be my wife, and I can't wait to share life with you for the rest of our days. I'm going to work to make every day of our lives better than the day before. I want a family with you. This is nuts! I've known you for a week, yet I'm so resolved. Every time I see you I'm in awe of your beauty, which is only rivaled by your sweetness. I could literally stare at you for hours on end.

> *I'm blown away by your strength. To know the journey you've been on and to see where you are amazes me. I have such admiration and respect for you. I want to see you reach every goal you have for the store and beyond. You will never have to worry about sacrificing what you've started because I want it for you almost as much as you do.*
>
> *You give me such peace and certainty about my life and all I've been through. I believe you are my natural example of God's ability to restore. I don't regret anything I've been through because I believe it has prepared me to be what you deserve. I mean that with all my heart. I'm so happy I have the wisdom that only extreme pain can give so that I can turn it into something wonderful.*
>
> *I'm not going to say I don't know where this is going because I do. I know it. I don't doubt it for one second. I never thought I would want to be with anyone again. I never thought I would consider starting a family again. With you, it's like I have a second chance at life. I can't begin to describe how excited I am. Though I haven't told you yet, and I'm going to do my best to wait, I love you, Jemilynn. I know I already love you. I know I'm going to love you forever. I know I was made to love you. I know loving you forever is going to be one of the greatest gifts God has ever given me.*

I could never have written that unless I took a chance. I stepped out. I tell you this story because I guarantee there are things in life you have endured that have completely snuffed out the dreams and ambitions you once had. Whether it's a failed marriage, a failed business, or just the fact that things are not working out in some area of life—all these things can cause you to avoid the pain. Don't do it.

I'm going to let you in on a little secret. You know what's on the other side of fear? Nothing. There's nothing there. Push through it. Be willing to evaluate whether your thoughts and feelings are real, or if they are conditioned thoughts and beliefs neurologically built for self-protection.

Don't waste the pain in your life. Use it to fortify your strength. Use is to fuel your courage to live bigger and deeper than ever before. If love has broken your heart, overcome it by loving even bigger and harder.

Before Jemilynn, I could not conceive of marrying again. I had been through too much pain. I was cynical and jaded. I just didn't see the point. However, had I not stepped out and given just a little oxygen to the idea that maybe I'd regret being alone, I would have let a great catastrophe lead to the greatest catastrophe of all: not making Jemilynn my wife.

If you are down in the valley, you are courageously standing where the mere thought of being keeps most people from reaching their potential. They are so afraid of ending up where you are, but look at you! You are there, and you are surviving. As you'll see from the other people whose stories I'll share, nothing pushes you like having nothing to lose.

NOTHING TO LOSE

I watched this one from a front-row seat. Kim interviewed with me several years ago when I was a broker. At the time, she was working for someone else—a job she had held for over 12 years. It should also be noted Kim was very good at her job. However, there were several things missing, and she decided she would change careers and get her real estate license. That's when Kim came into my life. She told me her background, and we developed a long term plan to get her license while working at her present job. If and when she felt she could make a living selling real estate, she would come on board full time. Kim would call me almost daily with updates on her progress in her classes, as well as with questions about the business.

Then her boss found out she had received her real estate license and fired her on the spot! Kim and her family were relying heavily on her income, so this news was a blow. She was in tears when she told me what happened. Our plan to ease into the business changed to her being thrown headfirst into a new career. I assured her we would just have to make certain she was successful that much earlier!

In the first three months, I let her assist me on a couple of my listings. By month four, she was off to the races. Kim shot to the top one percent of all real estate agents in the Greater Tyler Association of Realtors. She absolutely loves what she does for a living, and her income has multiplied five times! What seemed to be a catastrophic event only served to push her into a situation where she had to succeed.

GOING FOR IT

Are you in a similar crisis situation right now? Do you wake up every morning and feel as if you have an elephant sitting on your chest? What are you going to do about it? You might just be in the greatest spot you could ever be. Having nothing leaves you with nothing to lose. You will never go for it until your desire for what you might gain outweighs the fear of what you might lose.

When trainers bring baby elephants into a circus, they teach them to stay put by tying a small rope to the elephant's leg and driving a stake in the ground. As the elephant grows, the rope stays the same length, with the same stake. By the time the elephant is full size, he could easily yank the stake and rope right out of the ground. However, he doesn't know that! I wonder what the elephant would do if he knew he could pop the stake and run free. The trainer won't tell him, because he wants him to stay put.

You can remove the stakes that are holding you back in life. Easily. You just have to decide that you're big enough and strong enough to remove them. You've believed for the longest time you could or couldn't do certain things just because "that's the way it is." I'm here to tell you that's not the case. Some stakes are in your life for good reason. Others are there simply because it's all you've ever known. Losing your job or your home could free you to live a better life than you ever imagined. Don't let fear bind you. You're free! In America, you are free to dream, free to build, and free to pursue happiness, so go out and exercise your freedoms.

SETTING YOUR DREAMS ON FIRE

The morning headline read: "Edison Sees Vast Plant Burn; Inventor and Wife Direct Salvage Work as Ten Buildings Go in $7,000,000 Fire." It was early evening on December 9, 1914, when Thomas Edison heard a fiery explosion. He ran from his laboratory and into the courtyard of the factory complex where he worked. The famous inventor stood helpless as he watched his entire life's work go up in flames.

After the smoke cleared, he told an astonished media that he simply planned to start over again the next day. He was 67 years old. Edison wisely said, "There is great value in disaster. All our mistakes are burned up. Thank God we can start anew."

Has your "factory" burned to the ground? Have you lost your job? Missed a promotion? Had your hours unexpectedly cut back? It's possible this devastating event represents a new beginning of something even better than the smoldering ashes of your past. How else are you going to look at it? To wallow in utter despair is not going to feed your family or make your car payment. It's definitely not going to help you live the life you were intended to live. Don't go down that road. Decide today that whatever you face, you will refuse to accept anything less than a better life.

Maybe your crisis hasn't happened...yet. But what would you do if your dreams went up in smoke? Some of us need to set our dreams on fire and see what happens. Will they go up in smoke because they were meaningless to begin with? Or will the urgency of the moment start a raging bonfire inside your soul for a new and better dream?

CONSIDER YOUR OPTIONS

In the late 90s and early years of 2000, nearly everyone was a Seinfeld fan. It was "the" show of its era. Kramer, Jerry's kooky neighbor, once had the bright idea to construct levels all over his apartment. Jerry, being the pragmatic straight man, immediately bet Kramer that he would not do it. Later in the episode, Jerry's dad asks Kramer how the levels are coming. Kramer replies that he decided not to do it, to which Jerry says, "Pay up!" He won the bet. But Kramer disagrees, stating that he *could* build the levels. He had just decided not to. Jerry argues that the bet was never whether or not he "could" build the levels, but whether or not he actually did!

Many people approach their dreams and ambitions this way and say, "I could do this or that if I wanted to..." You aren't going to win any bets for what you could do! The only thing that offers returns is what you actually do in life. There are only three options when it comes down to it. You either act on a dream, and it succeeds. Or you refuse to act and keep it all in your head. Or you act on it and see it fail. The last option keeps so many people from pursuing whatever passion burns inside them. Let's break down these scenarios just in case you find yourself in this predicament—so afraid if you step out and fail that the potential devastation has you stuck like Chuck.

Worst-case scenario

What's the worst that could happen? You strike out, and sure enough, you crash and burn. You fail miserably. Is life over now that you know what *not* to do? Remember Edison's example. Nothing could discourage the man. When asked about the number of failed experiments leading to his creation of the incandescent light bulb, he scoffed and said he had not failed—he'd simply made 300 discoveries of "how not to make a light bulb." So what if your dreams burn out? You figured out which dream not to pursue. As George Burns once said, "I honestly think it is better to be a failure at something you love than to be a success at something you hate."

I gave a rough draft manuscript of this book to one of my most trusted friends before I published it. I can count on him to be brutally honest. In his feedback, he said he wanted me to explain what I would have done if I had failed at my dream. What if my real estate business had crumbled? What if I never made it as a writer and speaker? Since I'm writing a book to convince people they need to push play and follow their dreams, he suggested I also describe what to do when the plan doesn't work.

The first thing I would like to say is "thank you" to my buddy, Jim. After all, if he believes that some readers will quit their jobs because of this book and go for it, then I must have a winner here! (I write this with my tongue firmly planted in my cheek.) But I have to be honest. I didn't dwell on failure when I started my broker business. And I don't think about it now in my new gig. I truly believe this is my calling from God. So many people sit around saying, "What if..." for way too long. "What if..." "What if..." "What if..." and beeeeeeeep they go flatline.

I could always get another job. Even if it was a job mowing yards, I could get a job. The idea of possibly moving into an apartment, mowing yards, and struggling financially for a while is not a real appealing one. Yet neither is the knowledge that I never tried. Theodore Roosevelt said, "Far better is it to dare mighty things, to win glorious triumphs, even though checkered by failure...than to rank with those poor spirits who neither enjoy nor suffer much, because they live in a gray twilight that knows not victory nor defeat." Granted, some are perfectly happy living a life of mediocrity. God bless them. It's just not for me.

A couple in Dallas once listed two homesites with me. I later learned they bought them as speculative investments. Not only did they turn out to be unprofitable investments, but the gentleman who bought them was about to lose his business. He is an entrepreneur who built his company up to 300 employees and was doing rather well at one point. However, due to some unfortunate incidents, the company was not going to make it.

As we visited, he revealed how the thought of returning to corporate America made his stomach ache. Even in the midst of financial ruin, this guy was looking for his next entrepreneurial venture. He realized he hadn't failed; he just learned from his mistakes. He was now wiser and more sure of himself than ever. While it would be rough, I knew he would survive.

There are only two basic needs in this life: food and shelter. It doesn't take a lot to get either. In your worst-case scenario, you might have to go through some penny-pinching and some pride-swallowing for a while. But if you truly believe you are destined to pursue your dream (and you can envision yourself living it out), then learn to hold loosely those material things you once held so dear.

Have a plan, but don't plan to fail before you even try! Rather, think about how you'll rebuild in case things don't go as planned. Malcolm Forbes said, "Failure is success, if we learn from it." You must go into whatever you are pursuing with the realization that there isn't such a thing as failure. There are only lessons learned.

Let's face it. If you stay put, are you 100% certain that you will be successful? Are you 100% certain you won't lose your job due to downsizing? If the answer is no, then take a shot at doing something great.

Best-case scenario

What about this scenario? You shoot for the stars and, bingo, you make it? The only thing you will beat yourself up for is waiting so long to take your life off pause and get going. That's the best-case scenario, and only you know what that will look and feel like in your particular situation.

There is a third scenario. Nothing happens. That's the worst-case scenario for me.

What if you reach the end of your life and your dream is still untouched? Like a gorgeous car with no engine, there's no way it will ever start now. Its time will have passed. What will you have then? You can't get back all the days you wasted putting your passion on pause. They are gone forever. That's the thing about time. Remember, it's like a bank account that gets filled up every day, but you have to spend all of it. Your time isn't like your wireless phone service. There are no rollover minutes. Once they're gone, they're gone. When I first set out on my own, I knew failure was a possibility. I even knew bankruptcy (one of my greatest fears) was a possibility. However, the fear of bankruptcy was eclipsed by the dread of one day being too old to see if I could try.

IT'S UP TO YOU

I heard a story about a little boy trying to trick his grandpa. He went to his grandpa one day with an injured bird tucked inside his hand and hid his hand behind his back.

"Grandpop," the little boy said, "What do I have in my hand?"

The boy's grandfather had seen his grandson playing near the injured bird earlier that morning, so he answered, "A bird, my young man."

Disappointed that his grandfather had guessed correctly, the little boy planned to catch him on the second question. He asked, "Is the bird dead or alive?"

The wise grandfather thought for a minute before answering. If he said it was dead, he knew the boy would let it go. But if he said the bird was alive, the young boy might damage the bird. So he said the most accurate statement he could and replied, "That life is in your hands."

Some of you have tucked your dreams behind your back, and you're trying to figure out what to do next. Whether that dream stays alive or dies is entirely up to you. No one can make the decision for you to take a leap of faith, change your life, move into a new career, or evaluate your life. You have to make the move.

Dreams have a way of resurfacing, even once you think they're dead. Remember that idea you had for your life so many years ago? Don't be afraid to jump out and pursue it. Put a plan into motion that gives your dream the ability to thrive. Don't plant seeds of regret. Plant seeds of action.

You likely have something in the back of your mind you know you would enjoy. You know it would be fun, and you might even make some money doing it. However, your ego is stopping you. For example, maybe you are terrified to tell your family you want to leave your law practice to work at a vineyard as a tour guide. Hey, I never said doing what you love means you start the vineyard. This is about searching out whatever life you want and connecting your heart and your passion with your vocation.

I was fearful before deciding to peck away at the keyboard again. I was nervous telling my youngest daughter that after getting my tail kicked in a Congressional race I wanted to pursue public speaking. I felt like I'd announced I was joining the circus. My idea was not a real job, right? My ego was constantly beating me up. Finally, I forced myself to tell people my dream. It became easier the more people I told. Telling someone made it real. It also didn't hurt that so many people encouraged me.

You shouldn't give a flip what anyone but your immediate family thinks anyway. You need to consider family because your decisions impact them, and much of your success depends on them. However, everyone else who is not in the hula hoop doesn't matter. That said, you will be surprised how supportive people are when you tell them you're pursuing a dream. You become a hero of sorts. After all, who does that? I'll tell you who. Very few people. It takes a tremendous amount of guts to be completely honest with yourself and pursue your calling. People admire that kind of person.

To not give a rip about the opinions of others is so freeing. What's startling is realizing that freedom has been there all along. When you don't care what people think of your car, your house, your clothes, or what you do in your spare time, you are then free to be whoever you want to be. This is terribly critical. You must listen to me and get your brain around this point. If you are willing to shake the chains of the perceptions of others, you will be able to achieve just about anything. Pursuing a dream often means sacrifice.

It's about embracing delayed gratification, and you know what? It's worth it.

There are some things you must be willing to get rid of to chase your unicorn. It's about letting go of present good to reap future great. Letting go is tough. There are many material things in life we are conditioned to cling to, such as some favorite jewelry, a club membership, or an expensive annual outing with friends. There is no shortage of "things," and if you're not careful, they can weigh you down when you're trying to gain traction.

Do you know the story about how to catch a monkey? You put a banana in a jar and set it before the monkey. The monkey will reach in, grab the treat, and refuse to let go. His fisted hand is too large to remove from the opening of the jar, so he sits there holding on to the banana until his captor arrives and scoops him up.

What are your bananas? Is it your house, for example? This is a tough one, I know. A house is a powerful social identifier of who we are and how well we're doing. Your kids may have lived there for many years. However, it's one of the biggest bananas you can let go of to pursue what's really important in life. What if you could reduce your mortgage by $500 a month? That frees up $6,000 per year to invest in your plans. Explain the decision to your children and include them in the process. Let them know you have a dream, and selling the house will help you pursue it. Explain how much their support and understanding means. It may be tough at first and they may fuss, but kids are resilient and they will adjust. Where Mom and Dad are is where home is.

You also might have to sell some stuff. I often do a banana inventory of my own. I know I have some bananas that I need to release. If I don't do it, I'll have to start making extra money somewhere else. Refusing to let go will take away from being free to pursue my unicorn. It's going to be tough, but here's what I know. Whatever I sacrifice today will come back tenfold in the future. And once I'm able to have 10 times whatever I release now, I probably won't even want it. I know this is true. Do you? Be willing to let go of the banana to free yourself to follow your heart's calling.

TIME TO GET REAL

1. Like a bad penny, our hopes and dreams have a way of resurfacing. What's your "bad penny"? Why are you not picking it up and turning it into a dollar?
2. Are you allowing a past experience to keep you from pursuing a better future? If so, name that past experience in writing. Now that it's identified, what will you do with it?
3. List every ambition you have. Now, list all the reasons they are just ambitions and not already part of your physical life. Start scratching off the barriers that only exist in your head and have nothing to do with anyone or anything else. When all that's left are real challenges like geography, money, and family, start devising a plan to make those obstacles part of the plan to achieve your ambitions.

CHAPTER 11

IT'S YOUR MOVE

"Without change, something sleeps inside us and seldom awakens. The sleeper must awaken."
—FRANK HERBERT

You don't have to jump ship to make this book useful. If you think that, you're missing my point completely. If you are in a large company and love it there, but want more from it, you can put some of these principles into play where you already are. You can even dream your future success in the context of your present company. In other words, set a goal to become an entrepreneur within your organization. If you can convince yourself that you are working toward something greater, even if it never includes leaving your current company, then you are ahead of the game. If your goal is to become VP of Research and Development so you can stretch your creative muscles, then get to it. Start planning. Start dreaming, and start making it happen.

This is a wake-up call to realize you can do infinitely more with your life and your career than you realize. You just have to choose to believe that. Stop overly concentrating on your so-called career and focus on your life instead.

INSIDE CORPORATE AMERICA

If you stay at your present job, you will have to press on and try to refrain from becoming too cynical with the political nonsense woven into the fabric of so many large companies. I'll admit I grew a bit skeptical about "corporate America." How can you not be? It's hilarious. Everything, from the gross waste of resources to the incompetence that abounds so freely, makes for a real-life sitcom. I love the TV show *The Office* because it is such a realistic satire of what goes on in offices all over the country on any given day.

For example, let's talk about the standard corporate meeting. These things are awesome. I remember my first few months in the corporate world. I kept wondering when the work was going to start. On my first day, I sat in an eight-hour meeting! Where was the work? I was dumbfounded, and I was only 22. I was naïve and had not yet mastered the art of pretending whatever we were doing in a meeting was important, so that no one would expect real work to get done. Seems to me that if the people in those meetings faced the insignificance of what they waste all those hours doing, they might jump out of a window.

Here's the typical all-day meeting agenda. It's usually held in a designated room chosen by the caller of the meeting. There's a table in the back with all sorts of healthy delights such as danishes, bagels, bottled water, and Diet Coke, the nectar of corporate America. There is also always a PowerPoint. Now, if the boss is of the 21st century, he or she actually knows how to create and operate it. However, most know just enough about operating a clicker to get from one screen to the next. And they can usually only make it advance, not go back. Want to see a pot-bellied, overpaid white guy freak out? Just set the computer's screensaver to come on when the computer has been idle for one minute, and then put a password on the screensaver. I've seen it happen.

Usually, the biggest thing that gets accomplished in these meetings is the scheduling of the next meeting. At first, I actually enjoyed these meetings. I felt as if I were getting away with something. I was getting paid well to sit on my rump all day long in a big air-conditioned building, drink Diet Coke, and nod "yes." If I ever decided to make a name for myself, I would disagree for the sake of disagreeing (in a really intelligent way). Otherwise, I was just there for the Diet Coke.

I remember flying all the way from Houston to Orange, California, just for a two-hour meeting! This happened three times over a one-month period. What a waste of resources. The worst part is how we, as corporate schmucks, go around acting like it's important work. Again, we can't admit it's pointless nonsense, or we might find the highest window.

What about the buzz words? Those are an essential part of the Dilbert wastelands. For instance, the word "driver" is one of my favorites. Executives love to ask, "What's going to be the real 'driver' behind this implementation?" Then there is the catchphrase-to-end-all-catchphrases: "best practice." Do a search for consulting jobs on Monster.com and see how many job descriptions use, "establish best practices." It just cracks me up. Of course, I guess a job description that read, "find a way to do something better than it has ever been done" isn't quite as sexy as "best practice."

Oh, and Mr. Covey, thank you so much for "synergy." Every year a slew of phrases comes along, such as "KPI," which stands for "key performance indicator." Have you noticed everything is getting "crushed"? Don't worry, it's a good thing to "crush it." This one I actually like and have adopted!

Cullen and some of my other buddies at The Home Depot used to invent new catchphrases and buzz words, hoping they would catch on throughout the company. When it worked, it was truly beautiful. One of my all-time favorites (I still laugh aloud thinking about it) was "expanding the band of excellence." Isn't that a beaut? We agreed that the first one to drop this phrase at a random time during a meeting would earn points. Like Drew Carey says on the TV show *Whose Line Is It Anyway?*, "The points aren't worth anything."

Halfway through the next meeting, my friend Tobin told our boss, "What we really wanted to do with this project is to *expand the band of excellence...*" It was classic, but that wasn't the best part. We had also given birth earlier to the phrase, "Tearing down the floodgates." Think about that for a minute. If there is such a thing as a floodgate, tearing it down probably wouldn't be the best idea. That was the genius of it. It sounded like a statement of grandiose ambition, but it meant you were going to cause a disaster.

For extra points, Tobin added, "What we really wanted to do with this project is to expand the band of excellence…by *tearing down the flood gates.*" Not only did he pull it off, but he also stuck the landing. I mean, he deadpanned it. It was truly a sight to behold. Yes, there are a few things I miss about the corporate world, and this is one of them. It can be a fun place if you turn the cynicism into laughter. However, that's no reason to stay in it forever.

IT'S YOUR MOVE

At some point, you are going to have to make a decision. Are you going to keep doing things as you always have, expecting a different result? Or are you going to step out?

I'll never forget when a physician friend of mine faced a huge career decision. The group he was a partner in was imploding. Some partners were leaving to become hospital staff physicians, some were staying, and most of them were busy looking out for themselves. My friend agonized for months about whether or not he should remain a part of the group. He was a Christian and would often call me to talk about the decision he had to make. He had a lot on the line. My friend had helped build this practice and had a lot of equity in the group. He also had a very comfortable life in Tyler. His wife loved living in Tyler and didn't want to leave.

Sometimes we give ourselves way too much credit in the decision-making process. We think we know what's going to happen once a choice has been made, yet in reality, we have no clue. We can trace what we assume will be the consequences of a particular decision only so far. Don't believe me? Remember Steve Irwin, a professional diver and animal expert who dove too close to a stingray that took his life? Based on his experience from thousands of similar dives and hours in the water with stingrays, he thought he knew what would happen. No big deal. But he was wrong about that costly decision, and he died.

How about kids who refuse to jump off the high dive? They think they know what will happen—it will hurt! One day they get up the nerve to jump and find out it's exhilarating. And guess what? It doesn't hurt! We give ourselves too much credit for what we think we know.

One day when my doctor friend and I were talking about his decision, I had a revelation. It occurred to me that he had two doors to walk through: door "A" and door "B." We tend to think it's all up to us to choose the right door and deal with the consequences on the other side. We do this even when we have prayed with fervor before walking through the door. I explained to him that just because he chose door "A" God would not say, "Well, good luck with that. I'm going to stay behind because I wanted you to choose door B."

That's not how it works.

I want to dispel a myth as it relates to God when making this sort of decision. I often see people in a stalemate because they are so fearful they aren't following God's will. They become anxious and think if they make a move, it won't be what God wanted them to do. Therefore, they won't be successful. Nonsense! God does give us a choice, and he promises to be there with us no matter what. Sometimes after our less-than-wise decision, he says, "Oh! So that's the door we are going to go through…" Still, he's there waiting for you on the other side. He has promised, "I will never leave you nor forsake you."

There's no caveat that says, "I'm there…unless you make a bad career move." No, he's there no matter what.

I know some of you aren't Christians, and I keep acknowledging that so that you won't think I've forgotten you're in the room, too. I'm thrilled you're here, and if you walk up to me one day and tell me you're one of my non-believer friends, you will receive the same warm welcome any fellow Christian would receive. I'm truly grateful for you indulging my faith as you plug through this read. By the time you put this book down, I want you to start making some decisions. I want you to grab the remote control, push play, and choose to live, not just wait to die.

Don't give yourself so much credit. You do not know what's going to happen...even if you think you do.

QUESTIONS TO ASK BEFORE MAKING DECISIONS

Andy Stanley, who is also pastor of North Point Community Church in Alpharetta, Georgia, recommends asking three questions before making big decisions. Let's unpack each one he suggests and see what we can learn about making the right move.

"Are you being honest with yourself?"

You may think you are being honest, but you need to make certain. We often rail about our miserable circumstances, yet we are responsible for much of what's happened. When we are children, we only look at jobs based on the work itself. Kids who dream of being a firefighter, police officer, or doctor want to fight fires, arrest the bad guys, or heal sick people. We don't think about the money, fame, or fortune we will gain. At that age, we are more focused on the "doing" than the "getting." When we grow older, we lose that focus. All we care about is the "getting." As a result, we often hate the "doing" to the point that all the "getting" in the world will never make us happy. Take an honest look at the decisions you've made thus far that were more about "getting" than the significance of what you are "doing."

When I realized I was never going to be happy working for "the other guy," I had to start being honest about what mattered most to me. Remember Kim, who was miserable in her low-paying job, though she was very good at it? She stepped out, got into real estate, is now making a lot of money and is much happier for it. Oh, I can hear you now, "Wait a tic, Jason! You said it wasn't about money!" Cool the jets, turbo. I told you it wasn't about money for me. Money was a big part of why Kim wasn't living life to the fullest, so she needed to match her talents with the possible rewards they afforded her. Once that happened, it was on like Donkey Kong.

When you are honest with yourself, you may find you only thought you knew what you wanted, but you had no clue. This is going to be hardest for the guy or gal pulling down $500,000 dollhairs a year. That's enough money to convince yourself it's okay to put what you really want to do with your life on pause. That's enough money to be content sitting in life's waiting room waiting to die, instead of getting out and really living. If your whole life is built around the farce that you need all the garbage half a million a year gives you, you face the biggest decision of all. When you are really honest with yourself, you will realize all the changes that need to take place in order to be fulfilled.

"What story do you want to tell?"

I love this question. In fact, it's my favorite. I love telling my story. It's a good one. Hey, I'm writing a book about it, so I must like it. But let's start writing your story. If you were to share your story with a group right now, how would it go? What compelling reasons would you give for doing what you do for a living? What would you say about your family and your time with them? Would you be able to give examples of the things you love most in life and enjoy doing the most? Would it be a story you would be interested in hearing, as well as telling?

Do me a favor. I want you to write your story as it is now. If there are good parts, then write how good it is. If things are bad, then write how bad they are. If you are amazingly charming, write it. If you have a horrible sense of humor and repel people, write it. If you are filthy, stinking rich, write it. If you are dirt poor, write it. Above all, be honest. While you're at it, pay attention to your stomach when you write. See if you can sense the tingle of satisfaction on a Christmas morning or the burn of anxiety from witnessing a car wreck. Make a note of these physical reactions. Next, rewrite the story to remove all the car wrecks. What changes would need to be made? You may write your story and find it's one big car wreck. I've been there. I know what that's like. It's awful, but we have to start somewhere. There is no room for denial. This isn't one of those deals where you say you're on a diet in front of friends and then scarf Twinkies when you're home and no one's looking. Nope, this is the time to be completely real, because only you are going to see this story. Lying to yourself will only keep you from getting to the ultimate life of joy we are looking for.

"Is there tension that needs attention?"

Is there something inside you that is quietly saying, "Listen to me..."? If so, have you been ignoring this voice? A good ol' fashion Jesus freak, such as yours truly, believes this could well be the voice of God gently guiding you. For the non-religious, not-sure-ist, and the "no way there's a Yahweh" folks out there, I suppose you would call this your "gut." You need to give attention to this little voice. It rarely lies. If it does lie, it's not from God.

I've failed miserably at doing this more than once. While getting my MBA has had its benefits, it also had its drawbacks. It was terribly difficult on my daughters when I drove two hours to Dallas for class from Tyler. I missed a lot of soccer games and was very stressed at home. It was also a massive financial burden. I can tell you without hesitation everything in my gut told me not to pursue my MBA. It was vanity toying with me. I went ahead anyway, and I suffered, along with gaining the benefits. Which one will outweigh the other is yet to be seen.

Another gut-ignoring moment was when I ran for Congress. Everything in me told me not to do it. I didn't even want to be a Congressman. However, I felt duty-bound. When people you love, trust, and admire tell you to represent them in Congress, it gets to you. Further, as my counselor once said, I have a bit of a hero complex. The run was a colossal mistake. It cost me almost a year of income and drained a ton of my personal cash. It was exhausting and in a word, miserable. I hated every second of it, just as my gut had indicated I would.

My daughter Abby once said, "You know, people are funny. A lot of times, they know what they want...but they say they don't know. Even though they really do know all along." This is so true. Many of you know exactly what decision(s) you need to make to start living your life to the fullest, and yet you won't do it. If you do make a decision, and the tension is still there, then you're not listening.

You run the risk of becoming numb to that tension. If you constantly ignore the tension or little voice nudging you along, then before long it will lose its effectiveness. If you are reading this and your mind is flooded with steps you know you could take right now to be more fulfilled, and yet you aren't doing it, I have to ask (in a nice way, of course), "What is your problem?"

There are going to be moments when you face some internal tension and doubt, even when you move forward. Get to the root of the tension. Acknowledge it and deal with it. Don't sit in a holding pattern until the tension is completely removed. Take your finger off the pause button! Just be real with the apprehension and doubt, figure out what the small voice inside is trying to tell you and deal with it. Sure, stepping out might not work. You may have a setback. But man, what if it does work. There's only one way to find out.

TIME TO GET REAL

1. At the top of a sheet of paper list your single greatest ambition. Now, imagine organizing your life in a way to make it possible to pursue. List in column A all your "what if" concerns if it doesn't work out. (What if I go broke? etc.) List in column B all of your "what if" outcomes if it does work out. (What if I make a lot of money? etc.) Which list is the longest? Pay attention to your neural-responses. Does the fear of the negative outcomes feel strongest or the feeling of elation from the benefits? Be honest with yourself.
2. Have you truly articulated to yourself or anyone else what it is you really want from life? If not, do it in writing now.
3. Start writing the story of your life. I'm not asking for a full bio, just an inventory of sorts. Next, write about the life you want. If you're

writing about the past and some "I should've done this or that" pops up, bring it forward into the future. Why can't you do it now? Seriously! Just because you didn't do it then doesn't mean you can't do it now in 100% of the cases.

CHAPTER 12

ESTABLISH YOUR "TRIBE OF MENTORS"

First, let me acknowledge I took the idea of a "Tribe of Mentors" from Tim Ferriss who authored the book bearing that very title. I find it appropriate this chapter should include a nod to Tim since he sits squarely at the center of my metaphorical tribe. I'll give more color to my thoughts and admiration of Tim a bit later. However, I first want to explain my interpretation of what it means to have a tribe of mentors and put my own spin on it.

Humans are incredibly gifted and complex machines. The power of even the dumbest human brain is simply astounding. I'm continuously blown away by the ability to think, create, and execute that certain humans possess. Zig Ziglar said, "Success leaves clues." Therefore, given the genius that is out there readily available for us to investigate, why would we not seek clues from others about the mystery of self-improvement and problem solving?

So many thought leaders of today have podcasts, blogs, vlogs you name it. I feel as if I know my tribe. I know so much about their lives and their achievements because of the vast volume of media that exists today. There's something very exhilarating and inspiring about watching those who perform at the top of their game and seem to have the playbook of life all but mastered. They remind me how much I too am capable of doing.

If someone has done whatever it is you want to do, chances are good you can do it also. You just have to crack the code for what made them successful. For instance, I think Elon Musk is a genius, and few would disagree. However, I don't think it's his genius that made him what he is today. It's his amazing ability to dream and consider ideas far beyond what most people think is possible. So while I may not be as smart as Musk in the academic sense, I know I can train myself to dream bigger and more often. While many in Silicon Valley are wondering how to develop the next cool app, Musk is considering how to colonize Mars. That's a huge difference. Who ever thought of actually creating a commercial space program? Musk did. That's who.

So what I would like to do is introduce you to my tribe of mentors and let you know the role they have played and continue to play in my life. I'm forever grateful for the intelligent designer of these humans. These folks inspire me, humor me, help me stay healthier, and most of all, remind me what's possible in life.

MEMBER 1: TIM FERRISS (WWW.TIM.BLOG)

I first discovered Tim Ferriss through his wildly successful book *The 4-Hour Workweek*. I read how this guy, who was just a couple years younger than me, had figured out how to run his company from any corner of the world, become a national kickboxing and salsa champion, and live on his own terms. But the book isn't how I really came to respect and admire Tim. It was his podcast. I can't prove this, but I think all of us owe Tim a world of gratitude. If you're reading this book, you are most likely a high achiever who is thoughtful and interested in peak performance. Tim, more than any other early successful podcast personality, and I've been listening since Tim was just getting started, has brought the art of the long-form interview to mainstream listeners. On the outside chance you've never listened to the *Tim Ferriss Show*, please do yourself a favor and listen.

Why should you listen? Well, thanks to Tim, I feel as if I personally know Arnold Schwarzenegger, Whitney Herd, Jon Favreau, Vince Vaughn,

Seth Godin, and others. Now, here's what I mean when I say I "know" these folks. I know Arnold Schwarzenegger grew up in a house without indoor plumbing and made his first million in real estate, not acting or bodybuilding. Whitney Herd, the co-founder of Tinder and Bumble, is married to a guy in Tyler where I live. Jon Favreau wasn't sure one of the greatest movies of all time, *Swingers*, would ever be made. Vince Vaughn's dad was an incredible toy salesman Seth Godin makes oat-flavored vodka and brews coffee every morning, even though he drinks neither. The point is I know these people on a seemingly personal level.

I love the closeness Tim has allowed me to have to these people. Through his interviews with famous people, we gain a glimpse of their humanity and the common denominators that make these peak performers, well, peak performers. Thank you, Tim.

As for Tim himself, he's incredibly thoughtful and never satisfied with where he is in life. He is a constant work in progress. Tim's books are documented experiments and data repositories of everything from what you should eat before sex, what you should not do before going to bed, what you should eat first thing in the morning, how you can become a speed reader, how you can learn anything in a ridiculously short amount of time, and the list goes on. Another thing that I love about Tim's podcast is there are no politics. He reminds us that great is great, no matter one's ideology. As someone who has very strong political opinions, it has caused me to see and appreciate the greatness of other aspects of one's life beyond our political differences.

Tim's guests are people who upon their birth were very similar to you and me. They just made some different decisions along the way, hit some home runs, recovered from strikeouts, and collected enough victories to be something unusually successful. I really can't say enough about Tim and his podcast. Though I have never met and quite possibly never will meet him, I feel I owe him a debt of gratitude for his inspiration. I'm not too proud to say that, while I'm a few years older than Tim, I'd like to be like him when I grow up.

MEMBER 2: TONY ROBBINS (WWW.TONYROBBINS.COM)

This guy is an animal. Good lord, there simply isn't enough to be said about this literal and figurative giant of a man. I grew up watching Tony Robbins infomercials. I can't say why, but they captivated me. This guy with a giant head, giant teeth, and giant energy lured me in. As an adult, I began seeing Tony as the typical self-help guru. Mind you, I didn't know much about him. My perception was purely critical judgement at its finest. It wasn't until Tim Ferriss had Tony on his show that I stopped and said, "Okay, maybe I should see what Tony Robbins is really all about."

First, there's Tony's background. He grew up with a less than perfect childhood. His mother was pretty domineering, and his father left while Tony was young. Tony grew up by most standards poor. However, there was something special about him from the get-go. While in high school, he started working a night shift as a janitor. One evening, Tony missed his bus home and walked something like 20 miles to get home. He was sleep deprived, young, hungry, and had to be at school again only hours after arriving home. Tony describes this incident as the genesis of one of his priming techniques that I have since adopted. While walking, he started saying to himself, "Every day, in every way, I'm getting better and better."

At a very young age Tony began pursuing a Ph.D. in self-education. He would go to a small store near his home in California and purchase self-help cassette tapes. He would also read everything he could get his hands on by authors such as Napoleon Hill, Norman Vincent Peale, Viktor Frankl, and others. Eventually, he found his way to a Jim Rohn seminar. Rohn, an American entrepreneur and motivational speaker, would eventually become Tony's mentor, and Tony would become a top salesman at Rohn's organization as an event promoter.

Before Tony was even thirty he was making a million dollars per year. He eventually went from living in a 200 square-foot apartment to the Del Mar Castle, which he first leased then later purchased. Before he was 40, he famously purchased an island in Fiji. It's a literal paradise and it's all Tony's. Tony has a reported net worth of around half a billion dollars. He is one of the most sought after life coaches and peak performance consultants and speakers in the world. His clients include Hollywood elites and titans of industry. Tony has clients who pay over a million dollars per year to consult with them.

This is a man who walks his talk in a way few have ever done. To label Tony Robbins a "self-help" guru is just not accurate. This guy is a scientist and one of the most well-read and studied individuals I have ever encountered. Sure, his massive presence gives him an advantage. However, the real genius and talent is what he does with it. This guy looks for every possible way to make life as full as it can possibly be.

If you think Tony Robbins is just a motivational speaking huckster, you're doing yourself a huge disservice. If people like billionaire hedge fund managers Ray Dalio and John Paul Tudor Jones, as well as athletes like Andre Agassi and many others, look to Tony for life enhancement, chances are you could benefit as well.

MEMBER: ZIG ZIGLAR (WWW.ZIGLAR.COM)

Who hasn't at least heard of this favorite son of Yazoo, Mississippi? With his Southern drawl and undeniable delivery, Zig Ziglar is one of the foremost legends of motivational speakers to ever live. However, it wasn't always the case. In fact, Zig was dead broke when he was 45 after being a successful salesman for a cookware company. His situation didn't stop Zig. He knew he had something to offer and would travel all night to get to a speaking gig, only to turn around and go back because he had no money for a hotel in the host city.

He was busy grinding it out for years, collecting and delivering stories in his unique way until he finally caught traction. With the release of his classic, *See You at The Top*, he firmly ensconced himself at the top of the keynote speaking circuit. By all accounts, not only was Zig an incredible thought leader and motivational speaker, but he was also truly a good and decent man. Zig is one of my standards to listen to when I'm on the road and need a pick me up. No matter how many times I've heard Zig, I glean something new every time.

MEMBER: ANDY STANLEY (WWW.ANDYSTANLEY.COM)

I cannot overstate my respect for Andy Stanley, the Senior Pastor of North Point Church in Atlanta, Georgia. He is the son of legendary pastor Charles Stanley. The way Andy has scaled North Point is nothing short of remarkable. To simply categorize him as a preacher is doing an enormous disservice to the legacy of this man. By every measure, Andy is a leader. His podcast, Andy Stanley Leadercast, is not just for church folks. Andy deals with practical strategies and insights every organization in pursuit of excellence can benefit from.

North Point started as a home group in 1995 then later met every other Sunday in rented facilities. In 1996 the church purchased an 83-acre tract of land and built a 2,700-seat auditorium. By the end of its first year, the church was averaging 3,000 in attendance. North Point Ministries now includes six campuses and has over 30,000 in attendance each week. One of the things that strikes me most about Andy is the fact he runs North Point like a Fortune 500 company. He and his senior staff are committed to sound training, growth, and excellent execution. I encourage any business leader to pick up Andy's book, *Visioneering*. You'll be glad you did.

MEMBER: VIKTOR FRANKL (*MAN'S SEARCH FOR MEANING*)

Viktor Frankl is the author of the classic book *Man's Search for Meaning*. In this book Frankl describes his observations of human behavior as a prisoner in numerous Nazi concentration camps during World War II. Frankl gives vivid examples of the immense power of the human mind and body and illustrates how crucial the control of the mind can be in these circumstances.

The greatest and most applicable takeaway is his observation on the power of having something to live for—a skill exhibited by some of his fellow prisoners who survived. When we have something to live for, our chances of surviving even the most horrific of circumstances greatly increases. He also taught me one of my go-to quotes, "Between action and reaction is space." If we can condition ourselves to manage the space between action and reaction, we will be much better people.

MEMBER: GARY VAYNERCHUK (WWW.GARYVAYNERCHUK.COM)

I've peppered Gary V's wisdom throughout this book. Gary is a first-generation immigrant from the former Soviet Union. He arrived here after his parents had saved enough money to go to work in Gary's uncle's liquor store. Eventually, Gary's father would open his own store where Gary would work long hours seven days a week before he became Gary Vee, who would found Vayner Media, a digital advertising powerhouse.

Gary was an early adopter of using YouTube as a marketing platform for business. While others were intoxicated with YouTube's narcissistic features, Gary was interested in speaking to the masses about wine, particularly wine you could buy in his father's store.

With his blue-collar, no airs approach to reviewing wine, he became a YouTube sensation. His father's business exploded, and the 1,700 square-foot liquor store became a 37,000 square-foot Wine Library. Gary has a remarkable story about unyielding hard work, dedication, and grit. His father didn't give him anything, and Gary often reminds people he remained just an employee throughout the entire time he was building his father's store.

I can also relate to Gary because we are roughly the same age, and we both cut our entrepreneurial teeth on trading baseball cards. Like Gary, I used to trade baseball cards and loved it like the air I breathe. I could tell you every stat of every major player in the MLB at one time.

Today Gary is a social media sensation, and his fame has nothing to do with wine. Instead, he has made a name for himself sharing his thoughts and views on building a business, having the right attitude, and most of all, the deployment of patience. This is what I learned from Gary Vee above all else. You must be willing to be patient. These days I realize the journey is fun. Whether I hit the *New York Times* bestseller list in one year or 20, I'm going to have fun getting there, and I'm going to deploy patience.

MEMBER: RYAN HOLIDAY (WWW.RYANHOLIDAY.NET)

Ryan Holiday is one of the most impressive people I know. He's smart, young, disciplined, and wise lightyears beyond his age. When Ryan was out of high school and about to enter Stanford Business School, he instead decided to become an apprentice. Who does that? Who in the 21st century thinks, "Hmm. I think instead of going to one of the premier institutions of higher learning, I'll become an apprentice and work for free." Ryan Holiday did.

He convinced author and philosopher Robert Greene to give him an apprenticeship. Eventually, Ryan would become the youngest Chief Marketing Officer of a Fortune 500 company with American Apparel. From there he went on to become a bestselling author of great reads such as, *Trust Me I'm Lying*, *The Obstacle is the Way*, *Growth Hacker Marketing*, and *Ego is the Enemy* to name a few. He is one of the most sought after marketers in the country as well, with clients like bestselling authors Dr. Michael Eades and Tim Ferriss.

I also learned much about the Stoic philosophy from Ryan. As part of my daily routine, I listen to and read his podcast and blog, *The Daily Stoic*. In these brief messages, Ryan draws on Stoic philosophy to iron out contemporary issues.

MEMBER: SETH GODIN (WWW.SETHS.BLOG)

Seth Godin is a marketing mastermind in a class all his own. Part philosopher and extraordinary entrepreneur, Seth is all marketer and one wicked smart guy. A Stanford Business School graduate and former Zig Ziglar protege, Seth can bring an idea down to its most basic essence. His daily blog is one of my favorites. Every single day, Seth writes a new entry. It might only be a few sentences, but that's because he's smart enough to say a lot with few words.

I also learned how to make honey oat vodka from Seth. I don't drink, nor does he, but man, it's a cool thing to know. In addition to Seth's blog, I listen to his podcast, *Akimbo*. It is full of Sethisms and great stories, ranging from the dawn of the space program to the history of early television. It's well-produced and always a fascinating learning experience. I love listening to Seth.

MEMBER: TONY HORTON (WWW.TONYHORTONLIFE.COM)

As I mentioned earlier, Tony Horton is the creator of the wildly successful home fitness program P90X. Since starting P90X almost a decade ago, I have never darkened the door of a gym since. I love Tony's enthusiasm, positivity, and his ability to seemingly defy aging. I still marvel that Tony was older in the first P90X program than I am now. The cool thing is he's still going stronger than ever and looks amazing. I can't wait to see what he's going to do next. I think Tony is the modern-day Jack LaLanne.

I can't even tell you how many times I've done P90X, but I know I will never stop. I feel better at 44 than I did when I started doing it at 34, and that's in large part to Tony Horton. I consider both Tony and Matt, my next mentor on this list, my personal trainers.

MEMBER: MATT WILPERS (WWW.MATTWILPERS.COM)

Anyone who has been around me for any time at all or has listened to the *Texas Titans* podcast knows I'm a huge fan of two things, Peloton and Matt Wilpers. Matt is a Peloton instructor among other things and has become my personal cycling and running coach. However, it's not just because of his knowledge of fitness and training. It's because he's a genuinely nice person. Much like me, Matt escaped corporate America to pursue his passion for coaching, cycling, and running. As such, he is now one of the most popular instructors at Peloton, the interactive stationary bike program. I've had the opportunity to meet Matt in New York, and he's every bit the kind and engaging person I expected him to be. It's rare a week goes by that I don't ride with Matt on my Peloton, even if he's in New York and I'm in Texas. I have no doubt his popularity is only going to rise. Mark my words. Matt Wilpers is a special guy, and you will hear a lot more from him in the future.

WHO ARE YOUR MENTORS?

I've only met one of these men in person, but it's of no consequence. They freely share their wisdom and craft for all the world to consume. All you have to do is look for it.

Sometimes when I'm down, I turn to an audiobook by Zig and get inspired to continue following my path as a speaker. When I'm exhausted and in a bad mood, I retreat to my garage where Tony Horton is always ready to tell a cheesy joke and put me through a workout. I've struggled with fear and regret, only to have Tony Robbins impart wisdom through my earbuds and remind me there are tools to combat these feelings. When I'm craving an interview with a peak performer to glean strategies from, Tim Ferriss is there with a new podcast. When I'm beating myself up because I don't have enough Instagram followers or downloads of my podcast, Gary Vee reminds me nobody will care what I do for at least a year and that looking at likes and followers is stupid. If I put in the work, and let that be the focus, the rest will follow. And then there's Ryan Holiday, who is an example of living in a peaceful simplicity. He helps make stoicism a part of my daily life.

I certainly don't expect your tribe to be the same as mine, but I encourage you to have one. Napoleon Hill once described a group of nine mentors he called, "Invisible Counselors." He writes, "Long before I had ever written a line for publication, or endeavored to deliver a speech in public, I followed the habit of reshaping my own character by trying to imitate the nine men whose lives and life works had been most impressive to me. These nine men were, Emerson, Paine, Edison, Darwin, Lincoln, Burbank, Napoleon, Ford, and Carnegie. Every night, over a long period of years, I held an imaginary Council meeting with this group whom I called my Invisible Counselors."

Having mentors is so much easier to do now, thanks to the Internet and social media. Ray Dalio is the billionaire hedge fund manager of Bridgewater. After authoring the book *Principles* where he outlines all of the strategies and methods for running one of the most successful hedge funds in history, he offered an app in conjunction with the book. At no charge, you can download an app that will help you make decisions based on the thought processes of Ray Dalio! Could anyone in the last century imagine being able to look inside John D. Rockefeller's psyche? Yet we have Dalio's thought process mapped out by the man himself as a way for him to pay it forward. I told you…we are living in remarkable times.

TIME TO GET REAL

1. List 5 people you consider to be peak performers and people you would like to emulate. Be sure at least one of them is local so you can meet him or her.
2. Meet at least one person on your list.
3. Do a book report (yes, a good old-fashioned book report) on at least two of the names on your list.
4. Find 3 qualities all your mentors possess in common. What do their similarities say about why you chose them?

CHAPTER 13

WANTED: A LIFE

"Always bear in mind that your own resolution to succeed is more important than any other."
—ABRAHAM LINCOLN

In 2004, while on a family camping trip, one of my best friends asked me if I'd be interested in going on a mission trip to China with him. The goal was to hike through several remote villages and tell them about Jesus. Almost without hesitation, I agreed. Sure, I wanted to go for the sake of taking the Gospel to the ends of the earth, but there was also a bigger reason. I wanted to take advantage of the fact that I had now carved out a life that allowed me to take such a bold trip. I would be gone for 14 days and didn't have to ask anyone for time off. It was my time to take, and I chose to take it. Little did I know this trip would change my life significantly.

It seems to me the most life-shaping moments usually come at unexpected times. That was China. I was pushed to the edge of myself the entire trip. I was hiking with two other guys when we found ourselves in a remote region of the Himalayas. I was dehydrated the first day out and spent the next three days hiking through some of the steepest, leech-infested bush imaginable. My sight grew blurry, and I honestly didn't know if I would ever see my children again. I went through so many emotions. By the end, I was angry at myself for being so careless with the life of my children's father. Before we finally made it out of the mountains, I was 15 pounds lighter and had not gone to the bathroom in three days!

I had to decide during this trek several times if I was going to lie down and die or keep going. I hope you're never faced with such a decision. The 50-pound pack I carried on my back felt like every burden of my life piled on me at once. However, I knew I had to live or die trying with all my might. Was this trip devastating? You bet it was. Was this near-death experience the best thing that ever happened to me? You bet. God often disguises enormously powerful blessings in the form of disaster. We just have to take a risk and see what happens.

TAKE A RISK

As I write these words, the unemployment rate is less than 4%. It was creeping up to 10% just a few years ago in 2010 during the Recession. People are now coasting in many instances. They are lulled by this good economy and can't fathom taking a big risk. Have you ever seen a want ad that read, "Wanted: A Life"? Of course, "a life" is a relative term unique to each individual, so I'm not sure how the ad would read. But that's what we all want out of this world—a better life. I wonder what your want ad would look like if you could live life just the way you wanted.

Missionaries have this figured out. They have decided they want their life's work to be sharing the Gospel of Jesus Christ. They abandon the idea of having to have a "job" in the traditional sense of the word and instead opt for doing God's work.

They aren't the only ones doing this either. What about rock stars? I know I'm going from one extreme to the other, but it's true. I remember watching a VH1 "Behind the Music" documentary about one of my favorite rock groups, Metallica. Yes, I said Metallica. When the band started out, they had nothing and were all living in a cramped apartment. They were so poor they couldn't even afford a loaf of bread for their sandwiches. It didn't matter though. These guys were living their dreams, not wasting a bunch of time at a so-called job just because that's what they thought they had to do.

I can read many of your minds. You're thinking, "Jason, rock stars aren't exactly the most responsible people. I have a wife and two kids, you know. Besides that, very few would-be rock stars ever make a dime at it." Here's the issue: you think it's up to you to provide for you! Therefore, you can't fathom the idea of living a life of absolute, purposeful, and meaningful joy that is not focused so intently on a "job."

If you've found yourself looking for a job, you may be so focused on the salary and benefits package described in black and white that you've forgotten what you should instead be looking for. It's not what you want the "job" to look like. What you're looking for is what you would like your "life" to look like.

THE PERFECT JOB

In earlier chapters, I described the type of life I wanted to live when I made my move to entrepreneurship. If you remember, I didn't write anything about the monetary gain I hoped this venture would bring me. After I started writing this book, I realized it was almost by accident that I determined I would look for a better life, not a better job. We all fall into that money trap. We say we want a job that pays "x" amount of money. We want benefits. Two weeks of vacation. All the criteria you list when looking for a job are really just describing the life you wish to lead!

For example, if you're looking at how long or short the commute will be for a potential job, think beyond the number of miles. It can't be as simple as, "I want a short commute because a long one is an inconvenience." Go deeper and flesh out the reasons *why* you want a short commute—those things that have to do with the shape you want your life to take. You don't want to waste time in a car getting to a job that takes you farther from the life you want to live.

If you have a family, you want to know you can get away at lunch and go to your child's school and have a meal with him or her. The commute needs to be shorter so that you will have time to drive your children to school in the morning. Do you see the difference? Something as small as the commute suddenly becomes a key consideration. You want a life (not a job) that gives you more time with your family, specifically your children. So start building the life that will allow this to become a reality.

Okay, I'm going to have to lay some scripture on you now. It just has to happen. I give you the following from the King of Kings himself:

"Therefore I tell you, do not be anxious about your life, what you will eat or what you will drink, nor about your body, what you will put on. Is not life more than food, and the body more than clothing? Look at the birds of the air: they neither sow nor reap nor gather into barns, and yet your heavenly Father feeds them. Are you not of more value than they? And which of you by being anxious can add a single hour to his span of life? And why are you anxious about clothing? Consider the lilies of the field, how they grow: they neither toil nor spin, yet I tell you, even Solomon in all his glory was not arrayed like one of these. But if God so clothes the grass of the field, which today is alive and tomorrow is thrown into the oven will he not much more clothe you, O you of little faith? Therefore do not be anxious, saying, 'What shall we eat?' or 'What shall we drink?' or 'What shall we wear?' For the Gentiles seek after all these things, and your heavenly Father knows that you need them all. But seek first the kingdom of God and his righteousness, and all these things will be added to you. Therefore, do not be anxious about tomorrow, for tomorrow will be anxious for itself. Sufficient for the day is its own trouble." (from Matthew 6)

This biblical principle is also something Stoic philosophers acknowledged as well. Seneca once wrote, "True happiness is to enjoy the present without anxious dependence upon the future, not to amuse ourselves with either hopes or fears but to rest satisfied, for he that is wants nothing. The greatest blessings of mankind are within us and within our reach. A wise man is content with his lot, whatever it may be, without wishing for what he has not."

While this may seem contrary to everything I've written, I think what he is saying is that no matter what happens, we can find contentment if we no longer focus on the anxieties of life. We need so much less than we realize. This is why this isn't a book about how to become monetarily wealthy. I honestly don't think one needs a lot of money to be truly joyful, once they discover the true meaning of their individual life.

Here's the point. There is a God of this universe who wants you to do one thing in your life. He wants you to seek him. I know some of you don't place any value on that because you don't believe in him. But unless you are just a rabid, tree-hugging environmentalist, you have to agree that we humans are at the top of the food chain. That puts a pretty high value on us and our capabilities. The chance that you'll decide to seek out a life of radiant joy and end up starving as a result is pretty minuscule.

It's time for you to put your life, not your job or your search for a job, under a microscope. As you look at your life close up, what things mean the most to you? Write them down. Stop and write about what a fulfilled life looks like to you. My guess is it's going to include some activities. Not many people fantasize about being a slug. What is it going to take for you to get to do those activities?

SO, WHAT DO YOU "DO"?

Do you know what question I hate more than any other?

"So, what do you do?" I can't stand this question. I don't fault the people who ask, but I despise it. This one, simple question answers so many others on a subconscious level for the asker. What most people are really asking, based on the society we live in, is: "Do you make more money than I do? Should I or should I not admire you? Are you rich? Are you educated? Are you important?"

These days when someone asks me what I "do," I would love to answer like this: "I spend every Saturday with my wife at our retail boutique. Every Friday morning she and I have coffee at the place we met. I ride my Peloton no less than five times per week. We create and cook amazing recipes with our youngest daughter. We travel to New York a few times a year. I read. I write. I speak. I live. Thanks for asking."

To me, it's like, who gives a flip? The question should always be, "How's life?" That's one of America's downfalls, and I don't talk much about America's downfalls because I'm a blue-blooded, patriotic, America-loving fool. However, one thing we have done in our quest for American self-reliance is to allow ourselves to readily identified with what we do more than who we are. What we "do" should just provide the means for us to be who we are and do those things that exhibit who we are. That's it.

WHAT LIFE IS

I know what has worked for me won't work for everyone. I get that. I don't pretend to have it all figured out as to what life is all about. However, I do know this. We're here, so we might as well enjoy it and get the most out of it.

Staying in a job so you can continue to live a life you hate doesn't make sense. Loving your job, but hating your life, doesn't make sense either. This doesn't mean you should finish this book, march in, and give your two weeks' notice either. Great things take time and thoughtful planning. That's where the change starts. You must first acknowledge there is a change to be made and that there is, in fact, a way to make it.

There is such a thing as work-life balance, but life is far more important than any work you will ever do. These two things should never be in complete balance. It's like saying we need to exercise as much as we rest. That's not true. We need more rest. Life encompasses all that's truly meaningful during this time on earth, not any job.

On the scales of time, we need to pile as much on the "life" side as we can, because not one of us is going to say at the end of the ride, "I sure wish I had worked a little more at that job I couldn't stand." But I can almost guarantee you we will say, "What I wouldn't give to have been there to see those first steps."

Life is family, church, Christmas, Thanksgiving, school plays, the Tooth Fairy, first steps, broken hearts, and the miracle of birth. It is finding salvation, losing a grandparent, buying a first home, and going to the nursing home. It is first kisses, "I do," and Happy Anniversary. Life is Thanks Dad, Thanks Mom, first puppy, and first old family dog's death. Life is up, and life is down. Life is bitter, and life is sweet. Life is dropping your daughters off at college and wondering where all the time went. Did I do a good job? They know I love them, right? They'll be okay, right? It's gut-wrenching, but that, my friends, is life. It's not crushing the big sale at work.

STOP WAITING TO DIE

The first time I ever thought about the difference between living and just being alive was when a friend of mine was dying. He had lost his ability to eat or drink. He could hardly speak and couldn't get up from his bed. He required around-the-clock assistance. Toward the end, I remember his son telling me he thought they were no longer keeping his dad alive...they were only prolonging his death. I agreed. Just because we're alive, doesn't necessarily mean we're living.

I will never believe this was all one big random incident, this thing called life. I will never believe the Rocky Mountains were just some random occurrence. Nor will I accept as meaningless the fact I get butterflies when I look at them. I refuse to believe the miracle of childbirth isn't worthy of amazement. I believe we were meant to live. All of us were meant to live, not just some of us.

Life may be so far removed from what you wanted it to be right now. There have been times when I felt the same way, but I refused to stay there. We only have a little time on this earth, and whatever you believe the reason for us being here is, I guarantee it wasn't so we could put everything on hold and wait around until we die.

Don't focus on where you are now. Concentrate on where you're going and how all that's happened to this point will work to your advantage in the future. The entire time I was on the mountain in China, I kept thinking about telling my story when I showed up to my next Rotary meeting! That's what you have to do. Look to the future. Will you give a play-by-play then about why your life didn't turn out as you wanted it to? I hope not. Instead, envision yourself telling others how you arrived at a life you once could only imagine, no matter how simple it may look to everyone else.

BE PREPARED FOR THE JOURNEY

Gary Vee once posted on Instagram that if you are working for yourself and you start working for a certain pair of shoes, new car, or something like that, you're screwed. Man, was he spot on. If you're saving up for a pair of shoes, then you can't afford the shoes. Keep that money working somewhere, do without the shoes, and tell yourself, "If five years from now I still want these shoes, I'll have them and more because it will be so much easier to attain."

I was exactly the person Gary talks about in my 30s. Just when I started to figure out how to make money, I started spending money. I was so stressed and frustrated most of the time that I would justify the purchases as a salve to soothe my ever-aching nerves. Today I no longer go into an office every day. However, I still have thousands of dollars' worth of boots and clothes. I used to buy suits monthly, even though I rarely ever wore them. I went through a streak where I bought a new truck every four months. I was so stupid. I didn't realize at the time I had fallen into the trap Gary Vee describes. Instead of focusing on what mattered most, building a sustainable business and enjoying laying the bricks, I wanted instant gratification.

I wanted to look successful. I wanted people to think I was killing it. The last thing I wanted them to know is that I was struggling. The truth? People weren't thinking anything about me at the time. Why should they? They had their own lives. It was a lot easier to go buy another pair of custom made Lucchese boots than hold a training session for my agents. It was a heck of a lot more fun, too. I also had this notion that if I had it today, I wanted to spend a little today. What if I didn't have the money in the future? That, my friends, is as stupid as it gets.

WHEN THE EXCITEMENT WEARS OFF

If your unicorn happens to be striking out on your own and building a business, it's very much like any other new job you start. At first you're excited. There is so much happening, and it's so new and fresh that you really don't notice the problems at the company. It's also like moving into a new house. You love the house, but on move-in day you notice there's a leaky faucet. "Meh, it's okay," you tell yourself. You'll get it fixed. However, six months in, you have a major plumbing problem.

It's the same with work. There's something about the six-month mark when something in your brain says, "Hey wait a minute. Is this really what you're supposed to be doing? Aren't you smarter than this? Shouldn't you be making more money?" It is ridiculous how this happens. Running your own shop is much the same way. It's like marriage to a certain degree. The purchase of the business or the ribbon cutting is like the wedding. Everyone is there. They're all pulling for you. Some bring you gifts. Optimism flows from every corner. You're on top of the world. The good vibes and endorphins show up without so much as the slightest beckoning.

Then something happens. The guests leave. The reception is over. There is no cheering section. There's only you and the real world that doesn't give a rat's tail whether you succeed or not. Get your brain around that right now. The world DOES NOT care if you succeed. The universe is indifferent, and you must embrace that cold, hard fact. It's up to you to make this thing work, and it will not happen quickly or easily or without some pain. It's at this moment that you need to push the hardest. You need to remind yourself constantly that there is no timeline. So you set a proforma that called for profitability in three years. If you're in year two, what difference does it make? Put your head down and grind.

Forty-three-year-old Jason would tell 35-year-old Jason, "Dude look. You're in your 30s. You're so young. You have over 40 years left to get this right. However, if you just focus and grind hard for ten years, you will be set. You may not be able to retire, but you will be in a position to act with much more freedom. Don't buy anything you don't need today because, if you don't do that, in the future you'll be able to buy ten of it without feeling so much as a finger prick. The strange things is that by then you won't even want it. Your priorities will have changed. Your wisdom will have grown. You just saved a lot of money and better deployed the resources in the future."

I repeat. Most of the things we buy today, if we're honest, we don't need. We just want them. The point is this. You have to be more interested in the journey than the spoils. This is about experiences that do not end up in garage sales. They don't linger in your closet as reminders of your past vanity. Experiences bring wisdom and color to your life. They are things you cannot put a price tag on. I'd give anything to be back at my first office purchased laying tile in the bathroom at two in the morning. Those were exhilarating times, and I cursed them, every one. How many times do we tell our kids, "You better enjoy this because it goes by fast"? It's the same when you dive off into your hustle full time.

Please, I beg you. Don't make the mistakes I made. Savor the moments. Welcome the stress, the toil, and the pain. Those things remind you that you're alive, and you're doing something worthwhile. You're doing something few others dare to do. If it hurts, it means you're growing. If it's hard, it means it's worth it.

Remember what retired Navy Seal and ultra-endurance runner David Goggins says, "You don't quit when you're tired. You quit when you're done." The moment you want to quit because the grind is hard is the moment you need to put a huge, freaking smile on your face and say, "Bring-it-on!"

You are so very able to handle much more than you can possibly fathom. We all have a finite number of journeys we will take in this life. Be sure to stop and enjoy the scenery along the way. Take note of the hard days as a way to remind yourself in the future that you've done this before. It's no big deal. You got this. Go crush it.

TIME TO GET REAL

1. What is your biggest temptation that gets you off track in life?
2. What immediate distraction must you eliminate to focus on your goals?
3. What large and small sacrifices are you willing to make now in order to have the best future possible?

SUGGESTED READING

The following is a current list of some of my favorite books, as promised.

The Magic of Thinking Big by David J. Schwartz
The Obstacle Is the Way by Ryan Holiday
The 4-Hour Workweek by Tim Ferriss
Man's Search for Meaning by Viktor Frankl
Think and Grow Rich by Napoleon Hill
Steve Jobs by Walter Isaacson
Zero to One by Peter Thiel
Finish by Jon Acuff
Walden by Henry David Thoreau
Meditations by Marcus Aurelius
Seneca: Letters from a Stoic by Lucius Annaeus Seneca

ABOUT THE AUTHOR

Jason Wright teaches you how to decide what you'd love to do with your life and figure out how a job can help you meet that goal. Jason escaped corporate America to become his own boss and is now in the business of helping others love life and accomplish their dreams and goals. He is available for speaking, hosting, and coaching opportunities.

Jason is also the creator and host of the highly successful *Texas Titans* podcast, featuring weekly interviews from influential men and women in every industry who are leading in significant ways all across the U.S. and beyond.

Jason and his wife, Jemilynn, make their home in Tyler, Texas.

www.JasonWrightNow.com

www.ingramcontent.com/pod-product-compliance
Lightning Source LLC
LaVergne TN
LVHW051603070426
835507LV00021B/2734